THE GREAT WOMEN SUPER HEROES

THE GREAT WOMEN SUPER HEROES

TRINA ROBBINS

KITCHEN SINK PRESS

NORTHAMPTON, MASSACHUSETTS

AUTHOR, COVER ARTIST
Trina Robbins

PUBLISHER
Denis Kitchen

EDITOR
N. C. Christopher Couch

ART DIRECTOR
Amie Brockway

DESIGNER
Lisa Stone

ADDITIONAL DESIGN
Evan Metcalf, Chris Shadoian

ART ASSISTANTS
Denise Clark, Eric Drzewianowski

ART AND EDITORIAL INTERNS
Leif Nesheim, Beagan Wilcox

INDEXER
Randy Scott

SENIOR VP, PRODUCTION
Jim Kitchen

EXECUTIVE VP
Scott Hyman

SENIOR VP, CHIEF FINANCIAL OFFICER
Dean Zirolli

SENIOR DIRECTOR, SALES AND MARKETING
Jamie Riehle

DIRECTOR OF LEGAL AFFAIRS
Dorothy Varon

NATIONAL DIRECTOR OF SALES
Eric Hyman

CUSTOMER SERVICE MANAGER
Karen Lowman

MANAGING EDITOR
John Wills

PROMOTIONS DESIGNER
Evan Metcalf

WAREHOUSE MANAGER
Vic Lisewski

Library of Congress Cataloging-in-Publication Data

Robbins, Trina.
        The great women superheroes / by Trina Robbins.
                p.   cm.
        Includes bibliographical references and index.
        ISBN 0-87816-482-0. — ISBN 0-87816-481-2 (pbk.)
        1. Comic books, strips, etc.—United States—History and
criticism. 2. Heroines—Comic books, strips, etc. I. Title.
PN6725.R59 1996   96-22413
741.5'973—dc20   CIP

First printing: September 1996 9 8 7 6 5 4 3 2 1

CONTENTS

ILLUSTRATIONS

CHAPTER SIX

90. Panel depicting Violet Ray and her friend Lucy Benson, from a comic book story featuring Ultra Violet, drawn by Dan Barry (*My Date Comics* no. 3, November 1947).

91. Splash panel from a comic book story featuring Atoma, drawn by Bob Powell (*Joe Palooka* comics no. 15, 1947).

92. Title panel depicting Violet Ray and her friend Lucy Benson, from a comic book story featuring Ultra Violet, drawn by Dan Barry (*My Date Comics* no. 3, November 1947).

93. Page depicting Violet Ray's transformation into Ultra Violet, drawn by Dan Barry (*My Date Comics* no. 3, November 1947).

94. Panel depicting Violet Ray's transformation into Ultra Violet, drawn by Dan Barry (*My Date Comics* no. 3, November 1947).

95. Three panels from comic book stories featuring Miss Masque, drawn by Lin Streeter (*Exciting Comics*, 1946 and 1947).

96. Panel featuring Blonde Phantom, created by Stan Lee with initial stories scripted by Otto Binder (1948).

97. Caricature of Syd Shores, artist on Blonde Phantom, drawn by Ken Bald (1947).

98. Splash panel from a comic book story featuring gal Friday Louise Grant, aka Blonde Phantom, and her boss, the private detective Mark Mason (*Blonde Phantom,* 1948).

99. Panel from a comic book story featuring Namora, the Sea Beauty, story and art by Bill Everett (*Namora* no. 1, August 1948).

100. Title panel from the comic book story, "The Terrifying Ghosts from the Unknown," featuring Sun Girl, the Mysterious Beauty (*Marvel Mystery* no. 89, 1948).

101. Advertisement for comic books featuring Venus, the Most Beautiful Girl in the World, and Sun Girl, America's Most Exciting Girl of Mystery (*Miss America Magazine* vol. 7, no. 12, July 1948).

102. Splash panel of Venus drawn by Ed Winiarsky (*Venus* no. 1, August 1948).

103. Title panel from the comic book story, "Hedy's Picture Problem," featuring teen character Hedy de Vine, drawn by Ed Winiarsky (*Venus* no. 1, August 1948).

104. Panels of Neptuna and Venus battling, written and drawn by Bill Everett (*Venus* no. 18, 1952).

105. Panel of a sea creature from the final issue of *Venus: Strange Stories of the Supernatural,* drawn by Bill Everett (*Venus* no. 19, 1952).

106. Panel of Gilbert Shelton's Phineas Freak (*Fabulous Furry Freak Brothers,* 1980).

CHAPTER SEVEN

107. Title panel from a comic book story featuring Janie Jackson, aka Tomboy, drawn by Jack Kirby (*Captain Flash* no. 1, November 1954).

108. Panel from a comic book story featuring Tomboy, showing the super-heroine in her secret identity as Janie Jackson, daughter of police lieutenant Charles Jackson, drawn by Jack Kirby (*Captain Flash* no. 1, November 1954).

109. Two panels featuring Tomboy chasing a criminal, drawn by Jack Kirby (*Captain Flash* no. 1, November 1954).

110. Panel featuring Superman and Supergirl from her origin story, drawn by Al Plastino (*Action Comics* no. 252, May 1959; reprinted in *Action Comics* no. 334).

111. Panel from Supergirl's origin story showing her in her secret identity as orphan Linda Lee, drawn by Al Plastino (*Action Comics* no. 252, May 1959; reprinted in *Action Comics* no. 334).

112. Panels from a comic book story featuring Supergirl meeting President and Mrs. Kennedy and being honored at the United Nations, drawn by Jim Mooney (*Action Comics* no. 285, 1962).

113. Panel with Supergirl and Streaky, the Super Cat; art by Mike Sekowsky and Jack Abel (*Adventure Comics* no. 400, 1970).

114. Panel with Comet, the Superhorse, declaring his love for Supergirl in a thought balloon (*Action Comics* no. 311, 1964).

115. Panel from the comic book story, "Wonder Girl Meets Wonder Woman," written by Robert Kanigher, art by Ross Andru and Mike Esposito (*Wonder Woman* no. 117, October 1960).

116. Panels featuring the entire Wonder family united in the comic book story, "The Return of Multiple Man," art by Ross Andru and Mike Esposito (*Wonder Woman* no. 129, April 1962).

CHAPTER EIGHT

117. Detail from endpapers for an illustrated book featuring Russell Stamm's Invisible Scarlet O'Neil (*Invisible Scarlet O'Neil,* Whitman Publishing Co., 1943).

118. Page from a comic book featuring reprints of the *Invisible Scarlet O'Neil* newspaper strip, written and drawn by Russell Stamm (*Famous Funnies,* 1947).

119. Page from the comic book story, "School for Crime," in which Invisible Scarlet O'Neil investigates the criminal activities of Mr. Malignant (*Invisible Scarlet O'Neil* no. 3, April 1951).

120. Panel from a comic book featuring reprints of the *Claire Voyant* newspaper strip, written and drawn by Jack Sparling (*Claire Voyant* no. 4, 1947, collecting strips from 1945–46).

121. Illustration from a book featuring Russell Stamm's Invisible Scarlet O'Neil (*Invisible Scarlet O'Neil,* Whitman Publishing Co., 1943).

122. Three panels from *Fantastic Four* comic book stories, featuring Sue Storm, the Invisible Girl, as she serves coffee, goes to a fashion show, and faints (Top, bottom right: *Fantastic Four King-Size Special* no. 4, November 1966).

123. Two panels from *X-Men* comic book stories, featuring Jean Grey, aka Marvel Girl, as she serves dinner and feels faint (Left: *X-Men: The Early Years* no. 17, September 1995; right: *X-Men: The Early Years* no. 2, June 1994).

124. Panel from a comic book story showing Marvel Girl fighting the Scarlet Witch; art by Jack Kirby (*X-Men* no. 11, 1965).

125. Three panels from *Avengers* comic book stories featuring the Wasp as she powders her nose, goes to the hairdresser, and applies lipstick.

126. Two panels showing the new "old" Wonder Woman, reminiscent of the Wonder Woman of the 1940's, drawn by Ross Andru and Mike Esposito (*Wonder Woman* no. 163, July 1966).

127. Panel featuring the Teen Titans with a new version of Wonder Girl (*Teen Titans* no. 22, 1969).

128. Splash panel of the new "new" Wonder Woman, at the opening of Diana Prince's mod-influenced boutique; written by Denny O'Neil, art by Mike Sekowsky and Dick Giordano (*Wonder Woman,* 1968).

129. Panels from a comic book story featuring Batgirl, distracted from a fight by a run in her tights; art by Gil Kane and Sid Green (*Detective Comics,* 1968).

130. Two panels from the comic book story, "School for Crime," featuring Invisible Scarlet O'Neil (*Invisible Scarlet O'Neil* no. 3, April 1951).

ILLUSTRATIONS

CHAPTER NINE

131. Panel from a comic book story featuring the Avengers and Valkryie, written by Roy Thomas, drawn by John Buscema (*The Avengers* no. 83, December 1970).

132. Backer board for comic book racks produced by Marvel comics, featuring Shanna, the She Devil; Lyra the Femizon; and the Cat (early 1970s).

133. Panels from the comic book story, "Come on in . . . The Revolution's Fine," showing Valkyrie leading the women members of the Avengers into battle (*The Avengers* no. 83, December 1970).

134. Splash panel of Valkyrie, who joined the Marvel superteam, the Avengers, in 1972 in a story by Steve Englehart with art by Sal Buscema (*Defenders* no. 4, 1972).

135. Two panels featuring Natasha Romanov, a former Russian spy who is the secret identity of the Black Widow (*Amazing Adventures* nos. 1 and 2, 1970).

136. Panel with the Black Widow and Spider-Man, drawn by John Buscema (*Amazing Adventures* no. 1, August 1970).

137. Splash panel featuring the Cat, drawn by Marie Severin (*The Cat* no. 2, January 1973).

138. Panel featuring the Cat, drawn by Bill Everett (*The Cat* no. 3, April 1973).

139. Penciled page featuring the Cat by Ramona Fradon, from the unpublished issue no. 5 of *The Cat* (1973).

140. Script page by Linda Fite for *The Cat* no. 5 (1973).

141. Two panels from a comic book story featuring Venus and the Sub-Mariner by Bill Everett (*Sub-Mariner* no. 57, 1973).

142. Splash panel of Ms. Marvel, drawn by John Buscema (*Ms. Marvel* no. 2, February 1977).

143. Cover of *Spider-Woman*, reproduced from original art drawn by Carmine Infantino and Steve Leialoha (*Spider-Woman* no. 7, 1978).

144. Splash panel from *What if the Original Marvel Bullpen Had Become the Fantastic Four?*, written and drawn by Jack Kirby (*What If?* no. 11, October 1978).

145. Splash panel of Storm, the first African American superheroine, drawn by Dave Cockrum (*X-Men* no. 96, 1975).

146. Splash panel of Dark Phoenix, penciled by John Byrne and inked by Terry Austin (*X-Men* no. 135, 1980).

147. Splash panel of Mighty Isis transforming from science teacher to superheroine (*Isis* no. 1, November–December 1976).

148. Panel from the first Black Orchid story, drawn by Alex Niño and Tony De Zuniga (*Adventure* no. 428, 1973).

149. Panel featuring Wonder Girl and Starfire discussing love (*New Teen Titans* no. 29, 1983).

150. Panels with Teen Titans Lilith and Starfire and a winged alien, Azrael; story by Marv Wolfman, art by José Luis García López and Romeo Tanghal (*New Teen Titans* no. 7, 1984).

151. Advertisement featuring Ms. Marvel, the Savage She-Hulk, Spider Woman, and Howard the Duck (*Variety*, 1980).

152. Dr. Bruce Banner, aka the Hulk, gives his cousin, attorney Jennifer Walters, an emergency blood transfusion, transforming her into the She-Hulk; penciled by John Buscema and inked by Chic Stone (*The Savage She-Hulk* no. 1, February 1980).

153. Panel featuring the Savage She-Hulk, from a comic book story written by David Anthony Kraft; art by Mike Vosburg and Chic Stone (*The Savage She-Hulk* no. 2, March 1980).

154. The Dazzler battling with the Enchantress; story by Jim Shooter, drawn by John Romita, Jr. and Alfredo Alcala (*The Dazzler* no. 1, March 1981).

155. The Dazzler emitting dazzling light; story by Jim Shooter, drawn by John Romita, Jr. and Alfredo Alcala (*The Dazzler* no. 1, March 1981).

CHAPTER TEN

156. Splash panel from the *Daredevil* comic book story, "Last Hand," featuring Elektra, Assassin; story and art by Frank Miller (*Daredevil* no. 181, April 1982).

157. Elektra in Bill Sienkiewicz's series *Assassin* (1986, left), and Frank Miller's *Elektra Lives Again* (1990, right).

158. Panels from the *Daredevil* comic book story, "Last Hand," featuring Elektra, Assassin; story and art by Frank Miller (*Daredevil* no. 181, April 1982).

159. Panel from the comic book story, "Bellyful of Blues," written by Bill Mantlo, art by Rick Leonardi and Terry Austin (*Cloak and Dagger* no. 2, November 1983).

160. Panels from the origin story of Cloak and Dagger, "True Confessions," script by Bill Mantlo, art by Rick Leonardi and Terry Austin (*Cloak and Dagger* no. 4, January 1984).

161. Panels featuring Dagger, of Cloak and Dagger, hurling living daggers of light; art by Rick Leonardi and Terry Austin (*Cloak and Dagger,* reproduced from original art).

162. Panel showing three of the four members of Marvel's Power Pack, a team of four young heroes created and written by Louise Simonson; the characters were designed by June Brigman (*Power Pack Holiday Special* no. 1, 1992).

163. Panel showing the transformation of thirteen-year-old Amy Winston into Amethyst, Princess of Gemworld (*Amethyst, Princess of Gemworld* no. 1, May 1983).

164. Panel showing Princess Amethyst in Gemworld, using her magical powers to overpower her enemies (*Amethyst, Princess of Gemworld* no. 6, October 1983).

165. Panel from the Airboy comic book story, "The Diary: Chapter One, Hushed Fields of Battle," featuring the Valkyrie; written by Chuck Dixon, art by Ernie Colón (*Airboy* no. 46, January 1989).

166. Title page from the comic book story "The Death Lights," featuring World War II aviators Valkyrie and Airboy, drawn by Fred Kida (*Air Fighters Comics* no. 7, 1944).

167. Page from the 1987 revival of Valkyrie; story by Chuck Dixon, art by Paul Gulacy and Willie Blyberg (*Valkyrie, Prisoner of the Past*, Eclipse Books, 1987).

168. Panel from a comic book story featuring Portia Prinz, a parody of Wonder Woman, drawn and written by Richard Howell (*Portia Prinz of the Glamazons* no. 1, December 1986).

169. Panels featuring the Blonde Phantom of the 1940s, revived as sidekick for Jennifer Walters in John Byrne's 1990's series of She-Hulk comic books (*The Sensational She-Hulk* no. 40, June 1992).

170. Panel from a comic book story featuring John Byrne's She-Hulk talking with Marvel editor Renée Witterstaetter (*The Sensational She-Hulk* no. 40, June 1992).

171. Panels featuring Wonder Woman from *Crisis on Infinite Earths,* written by Marv Wolfman with art by George Pérez and Jerry Ordway (*Crisis on Infinite Earths* no. 12, March 1986).

172. Panel drawn by Ramona Fradon from the 1989 *Wonder Woman Annual*

ACKNOWLEDGMENTS

Special thanks go out to Michelle Nolan, the girl with the most comics in the world, for the use of her extensive collection of golden age comic books. Thanks also to Steve Leialoha and Tom Orzechowski, for the use of their respective comic collections. More heartfelt thanks for their contributions to this book go, in no particular order, to Robert Triptow, Paul Hamerlinck, Jerry Bails, Ron Goulart, Gwenn Mercadoocasio, Rebekah Black, Bill Black, Aldyth Beltane, Nick Leonard, Frank of Comics and Comix, Joe Field of Flying Colors, Brian Hibbs of Comix Experience, Al of Al's Comics, Ilia Carson and Gaston Dominguez of Meltdown Comics, Peter Sanderson, Mark Wade, Joan Hilty, Paul Curtis, Vince Fago, Cortney Skinner, Pete Marston, Maggie Thompson, Donald Goldsamt, Bill Blackbeard, Greg Theakston, Jim Korkis, Tasha Lowe, Stan Lee, Roy Thomas, Steve Englehart, Julie Schwartz, Sheldon Moldoff, Robert Kanigher, Jim Mooney, Marc Swayze, Linda Fite, Ramona Fradon, Lee Moder, Richard Howell, Carol Kalish, cat yronwode, Mark Evanier, Sarah Byam, Sarah Dyer, Gregory Wright, Bill Messner-Loebs, Barry Smith, and the gang at Copymat.

AUTHOR'S NOTE
EXPLANATIONS AND DEFINITIONS

This book is called *The Great Women Superheroes,* rather than *An Encyclopedia of Women Superheroes,* so that I could include only those whom I felt to be the best, the worst, the silliest, or the most interesting. If you are angry at me for leaving out your particular favorite, I apologize. Perhaps you can convince me that I was wrong.

For the sake of my own sanity, I had to define superheroines as those comic book heroines who fit in at least one of the following categories: they wore costumes, had special powers and/or had secret identities. Sorry, but this leaves out jungle queens, girl reporters, vampires, and elves.

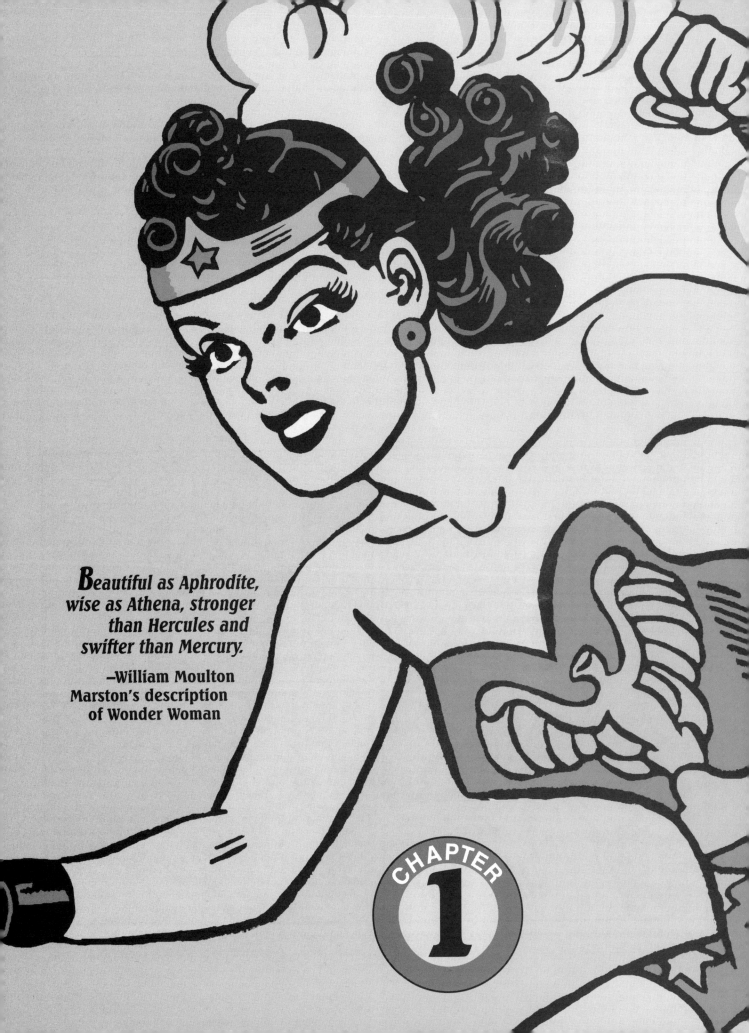

Beautiful as Aphrodite, wise as Athena, stronger than Hercules and swifter than Mercury.

–William Moulton Marston's description of Wonder Woman

CHAPTER **1**

In 1938 two teenage boys, Jerry Siegel and Joe Shuster, introduced their creation, Superman, in *Action Comics* no. 1, and superheroes entered the world's consciousness. Their story of a super-powered foundling from another planet had been rejected by every comic strip syndicate and comic book editor to whom it had been submitted before being accepted by Harry Donnenfeld for publication in his new *Action Comics*. Inspired by the energetic leadership of President Franklin Delano Roosevelt and the attempts of the government to alleviate the depression through the programs of the New Deal, the Superman stories struck a chord in the minds and hearts of Americans. Within a year, Superman had his own comic book; within two years, Siegel and Schuster's oft-rejected creation was also a syndicated comic strip appearing in over 250 newspapers, and the comic book was selling a million copies per month.

The success of the Superman character naturally led to imitation, and new superheroes popped up almost faster than a speeding bullet. In 1939, Batman emerged from his batcave to avenge his murdered parents in *Detective Comics* no. 27, and within a year he had his own book. By 1940, National Periodical Publications had concluded that superheroes were here to stay, and introduced the Flash, "the fastest man alive," in his own title, while DC featured superheroes like Hawkman, who dressed like a hawk and spoke to birds, in features in anthology books like *Detective Comics*.

1940 saw other comic book companies create their own superheroes. The Fawcett Company was the home of Captain Marvel, really a twelve-year-old boy who said the magic word "Shazam" to become invincible. Timely Comics followed suit with the Human Torch, who possessed the unique ability to burst into flame, and

1. In 1940, the first costumed woman hero appeared in comics. Undercover policewoman Peggy Allen donned a long, red, hooded robe and matching mask to become the Woman In Red; her adventures appeared in *Thrilling Comics* until 1945. (*Thrilling Comics* no. 13, 1941.)

Submariner, who swam up from the depths of the ocean to fight humans, but later switched his enmity to the Axis.

Accompanied by colorful sound effects like *Bam!*, *Crash!*, and *Pow!*, scores of other costumed heroes flew, swam, raced, and punched their way through the pages of comic books. Aside from their brightly colored longjohns, the one thing these heroes had in common was their gender. But the first costumed superheroine also appeared in 1940. In the pages of *Thrilling Comics,* undercover policewoman Peggy Allen decided she could do a better job solving crimes if she donned a disguise—a long red hooded robe and matching mask. Evildoers and the police she assisted had no idea that The Woman in Red was actually a police-woman, and thus she was also the first superheroine with a secret identity. The Woman in Red appeared sporadically in the pages of *Thrilling Comics* throughout the next five years, but unlike most of the superheroes who appeared in the initial burst of creativity that followed the appearance of Superman in *Action Comics,* the character was never given her own book and is almost completely forgotten today.

This was the plight of most comic book action heroines. None had ever appeared in her own book, and they were invariably short-lived, rarely lasting for more than three appearances before fading into permanent obscurity. Often they were merely sidekicks of the more important male hero. For the most part, when women appeared in comics they were relegated to the role of girlfriend, and their purpose was to be rescued by the hero. Girl readers could find little in the way of heroic role models in the pages of comic books.

In December 1941, a psychologist named William Moulton Marston reme-died this sorry state of affairs forever. As early as 1937, Marston and comic book entrepreneur Max Gaines had discussed the creation of a comic book super-

2. Dr. William Moulton Marston (1893–1947), psychologist, inventor of the lie detector and, with Max Gaines, the creator of Wonder Woman. He scripted her adventures from her first appearance in 1941 until his death. This photograph was probably taken during the 1939 New York World's Fair, at which Marston had an exhibit featuring his lie detector.

3. Marston also scripted the short-lived 1944 *Wonder Woman* newspaper strip, promoted by this comic book advertisement. (*Sensation Comics* no. 32, August 1944.)

By Charles Moulton

4. These panels from Wonder Woman's 1944 newspaper strip show the origin of her plump little sidekick, Etta Candy. In the first panel, from August 7, Diana Prince finds Etta in a hospital bed, unable to eat and suffering from severe malnutrition. (Today we would call her anorexic.) In the August 9 panel, she gives the girl a box of chocolates. Etta says, "Gimme–gimme more! Gimme the box!" The results can be seen in the panel from August 21.

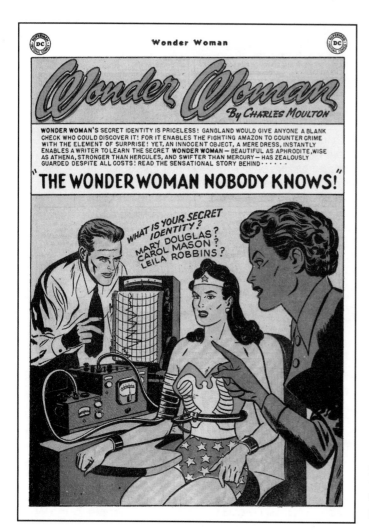

heroine. Marston is certainly one of the more unusual figures in the history of comic art. The inventor of the lie detector, Marston was a member of the Massachusetts bar, holder of a doctorate in psychology from Harvard University, a successful advertising man, and the author of popular and scholarly books and articles on psychology.

Marston and Gaines came up with several concepts that they hoped would attract women readers, including a female version of Tarzan named Diana (after the classical goddess of the hunt), but none was immediately translated into comic book form. However, in 1941, Marston's heroine at last debuted, first in *All Star Comics* no. 8, and one month later in *Sensation Comics* no. 1. This character was the Amazon Princess Diana, who became Wonder Woman when she left the land of the Amazons to become a costumed superheroine.

It had taken both Superman and Batman a year after their first appearances to get their own books, but less than six months after her appearance in *Sensation,* the Summer 1942 issue of *Wonder Woman* no. 1 arrived on the newsstands,

5. An ironic splash panel from a 1952 issue of *Wonder Woman* which links two of Marston's creations: Wonder Woman and the lie detector. (*Wonder Woman* no. 53, May–June 1952.)

JUDGE'S REVUE OF THE TUBE SKIRT

THE FIRST SHEATH-GOWN FOUND IT IMPOSSIBLE TO "NAVIGATE" CITY'S STREETS

THE SLIT-SKIRT HAS ALMOST AS DIFFICULT A TIME

BUT TO-DAY WITH THE FORTY-SEVEN VARIETIES, THE CROWD GROWS ACCUSTOMED

6. Harry G. Peter (d. 1958), who created the definitive golden-age Wonder Woman, began his career as a cartoonist for humor magazines like *Judge* and *Leslie's*. (*Judge*, 1914.)

7. Art by Harry G. Peter, from *Heroic Comics, circa* late forties, a comic book which related stories of real heroes.

and the amazing Amazon had her own title. At its peak, the monthly *Wonder Woman* comic book sold around two and a half million copies, and by 1944 she even had her own newspaper comic strip.

Marston knew exactly how to go about creating a superheroine for girls. In 1943, he wrote an article for *The American Scholar* in which he described the reasoning that went into Wonder Woman's creation: "It seemed to me, from a psychological angle, that the comics worst offense was their blood-curdling masculinity. . . . It's smart to be strong. It's big to be generous, but it's sissified, according to exclusively male rules, to be tender, loving, affectionate, and alluring. 'Aw, that's girl stuff!' snorts our young comics reader, 'Who wants to be a girl?' And that's the point: not even girls want to be girls so long as our feminine archetype lacks force, strength. . . . Women's strong qualities have become despised because of their weak ones."

Marston went on to describe the reactions of publishers to his suggestion that girls might want to read about and identify with a strong heroine: "My suggestion was met by a storm of mingled protests and guffaws. Didn't I know that heroines had been tried in pulps and comics and, without exception, found failure? Yes, I pointed out, but they weren't superwomen. . . ."

Although Marston's article in *The American Scholar* was published under his own name for an audience of his professional peers, indicating that he was proud to have been the creator and scriptwriter for *Wonder Woman,* all his comic book work appeared under the pseudonym Charles Moulton. The writing of his early *Wonder Woman* scripts was a family affair. Marston's wife, Elizabeth Holloway Marston, was also a psychologist, and she had a hand in the Amazon princess's creation. His son, Pete, sent in story ideas from college and was paid twenty-five dollars for each one that was used.

Writing his scripts in longhand, Marston combined his knowledge of psychology with elements from mythology and fairy tales to create the mystical Paradise Island, the homeland of the Amazons where men are forbidden to tread. Princess Diana's origin springs directly from classical mythology. The mythic hero is usually born from the union of a virgin and a god, and when the virginal Amazon queen Hippolyta desires a child, the goddess Aphrodite

8. In a three-part story set in "Shamrock Land," Marston surrounded Wonder Woman with the leprechauns and fairies of Irish mythology, and Harry G. Peter drew some of his most fairy tale–like art. (*Wonder Woman* no. 14, 1945.)

instructs her to mold one out of clay, then breathes life into the statue. Thus, Wonder Woman's divine parent is, in this case, a female deity, and little Diana has two mommies.

When Steve Trevor, an intelligence officer from the United States, crashes his plane on Paradise Island, he is rescued and nursed back to health by Princess Diana. She saves his life with the "purple ray," falls in love with him, and eventually takes him back to America. Disguised as an Army nurse, and later as Lieutenant Diana Prince, she stays in "the man's world" to fight injustice as Wonder Woman. With her she brings some accouterments of science fiction and fantasy: a magic golden lasso which compels anyone caught in its links to obey the lasso's holder, an invisible plane which Wonder Woman can contact telepathically, and a "mental radio," which resembles a small TV set in the shape of a Greek temple.

Just as one can't envision Lewis Carroll's *Alice in Wonderland* without the illustrations of Sir John Tenniel, nor imagine the world of A. A. Milne's *Winnie the Pooh* in any other way than that created by the Ernest H. Shepard illustrations, so Wonder Woman was defined for all time by her original illustrator, Harry G. Peter. H. G. Peter's art appeared as early as the teens, when he did cartoons for the humor magazines *Judge* and *Leslie's.* He also contributed some minor stories to other comic books, but nothing else approached the level of his *Wonder Woman* art. Working in a style utterly unlike that seen anywhere else in comics, perhaps because he was older than most comic artists, Peter lent an almost art nouveau air to the fairy tale–like stories. With bold brushstrokes he fleshed out Marston's Amazon maiden, giving her thick, curly Mediterranean hair, a strong, well-defined chin, and the slim, muscular body of an Olympic swimming champion.

9. Illustrator and comic strip artist Frank Godwin (1889–1959), best known for the strips *Connie* and *Rusty Riley,* drew two stories featuring the Amazon princess in 1943. (*Sensation* no. 19, July 1943.)

Marston and Peter were a perfect creative team—a rare occurrence in comics—and it is impossible to imagine one without the other. In 1943, for a reason we will probably never know (perhaps illness kept Peter from meeting his deadlines), the Wonder Woman stories in two issues of *Sensation* were drawn by cartoonist and illustrator Frank Godwin. Godwin was an excellent artist, better than Peter, and he had many book illustrations to his credit as well as two successful comic strips, *Connie* and *Rusty Riley,*

yet the comic looks wrong. It's beautifully drawn, but it just isn't *Wonder Woman.*

On Harry G. Peter's elegant pages, there are often entire sequences in which not one male can be found. *Wonder Woman* as written by Marston is, like Paradise Island, a woman's world. Women are always the strongest characters in the stories. The handsome but befuddled Steve Trevor exists because of an unwritten law of superhero comics: the hero must have a love interest so there will always be someone to rescue. He is the Lois Lane to Wonder Woman's Superman.

Even the majority of the villains are women. They are always very beautiful, and eventually wind up seeing the error of their ways, thanks to the message of love and humanitarianism that Wonder Woman carries to the world as she rights wrongs. In a 1947 *Wonder Woman,* Queen Atomia, the exotic, dagger-nailed ruler of an atom world, tries to destroy Wonder Woman. The Amazon princess subdues her and takes her to Reform Island, the Amazons' reform school. On the way her invisible plane flies over Starr Sanitarium for crippled children, and they see children on crutches. The flame-haired villainess asks, "Why are those children leaning on wooden sticks?" In response to Wonder Woman's explanation, she sneers, "Bah! Why bother with weak people?" But on Reform Island, the Amazon Mala puts a girdle of "Venus metal" on the Atom Queen, explaining that "While she wears it she will have new understanding!" And indeed, "No sooner is the magic girdle around her than Queen Atomia falls repentantly on her knees." She says, "This girdle makes me feel so different. It makes me hate all the evil things I've done!" Eventually the goddess Aphrodite herself welds the girdle permanently on Atomia, telling her, "I weld thy Venus girdle on thee with the powers of eternal love! . . . Forever thy heart shall overflow with kindness. Thou shalt ever be devoted to the worship of love, beauty and humanity!" Returning to her

10. A full-page comic book advertisement for Wonder Woman's 1943 campaign for the March Of Dimes. Any child who sent in a dime to aid in polio research received an autographed print of their heroine. The advertisement included a letter from the National Foundation for Infantile Paralysis to publisher Max Gaines, approving the campaign. (*Sensation Comics* no. 15, March 1943.)

Wonder Woman

Wonder Women of History

ANNIE OAKLEY
1860-1926

PLUNGED INTO A PIT OF POVERTY THROUGH THE DEATH OF HER FATHER, ANNIE OAKLEY, A MERE CHILD, FOUGHT FOR SURVIVAL. AN UNFRIENDED ORPHAN, HER FEARLESS SPIRIT CONVERTED THE MISFORTUNE THAT BEFELL HER INTO AN OPPORTUNITY—TO DEVELOP AS ONE OF THE GREATEST MARKSWOMEN EVER KNOWN!

AT AN OUTPOST CABIN IN OHIO, (1864, TRAGEDY STRIKES THE OAKLEY FAMILY...)

11. A continuing feature in *Wonder Woman* comics was *Wonder Women of History,* usually credited to associate editor and tennis champion Alice Marble. These three-page stories reinforced one of the major themes of the *Wonder Woman* stories: through personal development, any girl could become a wonder woman. (*Wonder Woman no. 21, 1947.*)

atom world, she informs her subjects, "We must love, not hate!" Finally, she cures the crippled children of Starr Sanitarium. In a last panel that demonstrates America's postwar faith in atomic power as a miracle cure, the children have thrown aside their crutches and are playing ball and leapfrog, while Wonder Woman says, "The atomic universe shall ever shine to help humanity—its radio rays healing children's diseases. . . ."

The most powerful humanistic message in Wonder Woman, and the one most constantly repeated, is that super powers are not necessary for a girl to become a superheroine; the Amazon princess herself does not really possess super powers. Her incredible strength, speed, and agility are the results of superior Amazon training, and with comparable training any woman or girl could become a wonder woman. This was

demonstrated not just in the stories about Wonder Woman herself, but also in a feature that appeared in every issue of the comic book, Wonder Women of History. Credited to associate editor and tennis champion Alice Marble, these short comic stories told about real-life heroines like Florence Nightingale and Amelia Earhart who made and changed history.

To prove this point, Wonder Woman sometimes brought her message to real girls. In a story that ran in *Sensation Comics* in 1946, she meets little Olive Norton, who wants to play baseball with her brothers, but is a failure. "Girls can't play ball! Olive's no good," says one brother. Wonder Woman consoles the crying girl, who has just struck out: "Let's face the facts. You're not as good as the boys. Why? Because you haven't practiced and developed your muscles the way they have." She continues, "You can be as strong as any boy if you'll work hard and train yourself in athletics, the way boys do." Olive returns to Paradise Island with Wonder Woman and undergoes a crash course in Amazon training. She succeeds admirably—Wonder Woman exclaims, "I knew Olive could be a real athlete. All she needed was our Amazon training"—and leaps from the invisible plane right onto the diamond where her brothers are playing ball. The new, improved Olive proceeds to hit a home run, rescue her brother Jimmy from quicksand, and even help Wonder Woman capture a band of spies.

The Amazon's sidekicks are women, too, mostly students hailing from Holliday College. In contrast, most male villains, like Dr. Psycho or the Duke of Deception, are grotesque and stunted creatures who are beyond redemption. Wonder Woman has to battle them over and over again.

This emphasis on the female has led a great many writers (all male) to comment on what they have seen as lesbianism in the early Wonder Woman comic books. As early as 1954, Dr. Frederic Wertham, in his critical book about the harmful effect of comics on children, *Seduction of the Innocent,* referred to Wonder Woman as "the Lesbian counterpart of Batman." This set the theme for future writers, like Jim Harmon, writing in the anthology *All in Color For a Dime,* who called the comic "a very sick scene." He wrote that Wonder Woman would "exchange hugs and kisses of delight with the readily available Holliday Girls."

Actually, in twenty-five Wonder Woman comic stories from the forties, I counted five portrayals of Wonder Woman embracing another

12. After little Olive Norton is humiliated when she tries to play baseball with the boys, Wonder Woman takes her to Paradise Island where she gets the training she needs to become a baseball champ. (*Sensation Comics* no. 58, October 1946.)

woman. Twice she hugged a little girl, once a dying woman. Princess Diana also often embraces her mother. Presumably this is permissible. Of course, what Harmon and other male writers are not taking into account is that women do show their emotions, and do hug. On the other hand, American men are notoriously afraid of being considered homosexual, and never touch each other except when playing sports. These writers also conveniently ignore their favorite super-hero comics, where the action takes place in an almost entirely male world. Marston understood that just as young boys tend to avoid anything female, girls

13. Wonder Woman's best friends are the Beeta Lambda sorority sisters from Holliday College. These women's college undergraduates, usually dressed in athletic outfits, are plenty tough, too. Here they give Doctor Psycho what for. (*Wonder Woman* no. 5, June–July 1943.)

14. William Moulton Marston included himself in a *Wonder Woman* story featuring Dr. Psycho. He appears at top left, and a rare self-portrait of Harry G. Peter appears above Etta Candy's head. (*Wonder Woman* no. 5, June–July 1943.)

of the same age are not interested in boys or men, and identify most strongly with other girls and women.

Marston has also been accused of filling his comic book stories with bondage and with male bashing. In his 1970 book, *The Steranko History of Comics*, James Steranko stated, "Wonder Woman delighted in beating up men." Similarly, Richard Reynolds went so far as to write in *Super Heroes, a Modern Mythology*, that Wonder Woman was "developed as a frank appeal to male fantasies of sexual domination"! In fact, the stories rarely depicted the Amazon princess using physical force on her antagonists, except in defense of someone weaker. In her own defense, she usually resorted to the Amazon game of "bullets and

bracelets"—deflecting the bullets with her heavy steel bracelets. And, rather than punching them out, she used her magic lasso to capture the bad guys and compel them to obey her. Compared to most male-oriented action comics, *Wonder Woman* was pretty nonviolent. In a 1948 *Wonder Woman*, Queen Hippolyta expresses once again the constant humanitarian theme of the comic: "Wonder Woman never relaxes her vigilance against those who seek to rule people by brute force! She teaches that love is the greatest force...."

As for the accusations of bondage, the fact is that in comics from the 1940s, if the heroes weren't getting tied up so that they could escape from their bonds, their girlfriends were getting tied up so that they could be rescued by the

15. "Shaz . . . mff . . ." Bondage in Captain Marvel? (Left and right: *Captain Marvel Adventures* no. 139, 1952; center: *Captain Marvel Adventures* no. 94, 1949.)

heroes. Some heroes got tied up more than others. Aside from the word "Shazam!," the most frequently used expression in Captain Marvel comics was "Shaz—ugh!," as little Billy Batson got knocked unconscious before he could utter the magic word that turned him into a superhero. This was the story's conflict. The poor kid would always awaken bound and gagged, thus unable to say the word, until he somehow managed to

loosen his gag, shout "Shazam!," become Captain Marvel, and bring the villains to justice. Still, I have never read anything about the bondage in *Captain Marvel.* Wonder Woman's situation was somewhat similar to that of Billy Batson. Symbolically, Wonder Woman could not break her chains if she had been chained by a man. So, in story after story, she had to find some other way of escaping her bonds and emerging victorious.

Most men who have written about comic book history are not particularly kind to super-heroines, but they seem to reserve their most

16. Captain Marvel Junior, Billy Batson, and Mary Marvel escape from their bondage by saying the magic word.

NOW I AM CLOSE ENOUGH FOR ACTION--

SNAP!

17. Like women protagonists of the movies and of other forms of popular fiction, Wonder Woman was often imprisoned or bound. Wonder Woman didn't wait around for a man to rescue her, but almost always saved herself with her own strength and intelligence. (*Wonder Woman* no. 34, March–April 1949.)

unkind observations for Wonder Woman, the longest-lasting and most popular superheroine of all. Les Daniels demonstrated his awareness of this when he wrote in his 1970 book, *Comix, a History of Comic Books in America:* "Masculine critics have viewed her [Wonder Woman] with a mixture of contempt and alarm. . . ." But then he betrayed his own masculine attitudes when he added: "In the hands of artist Harry Peter she was perhaps the least visually attractive of comic book heroines. . . ." He neglected to inform the reader by what standard he made this judgment, and one wonders if it was not the same standard Jules Feiffer used in his 1965 book, *The Great Comic Book Heroes.* Among his comments on Wonder Woman, Feiffer refers to his younger self as wondering, "Why was she so flat-chested?" Alone of all male critics, Feiffer had the self-awareness to declare, "I never knew they [girls] read her [Wonder Woman]—or any comic book. That girls had a preference for my brand of literature would have been more of a frightening image to me than any number of men being beaten up by Wonder Woman." Perhaps Frederic Wertham was correct when he wrote, "For boys, Wonder Woman is a frightening image."

Marston himself foresaw these reactions when, in his 1943 article, he described the negative reactions to his proposed superheroine. "Well, asserted my masculine authorities, if a woman hero were stronger than a man, she would be even less appealing. Boys wouldn't stand for that; they'd resent the strong gal's superiority."

But for generations of girls, the inspiration received from stories of the amazing Amazon is best expressed by pioneer feminist Gloria Steinem who, in her introduction to a 1972 collection of Wonder Woman stories, described "the relief, the sweet vengeance, the toe-wriggling pleasure of reading about a woman who was strong, beautiful, courageous, and a fighter for social justice."

Himmel, vot iss!! Dot black cat!

–Movie director
Garboil, in the first Black
Cat story, *Pocket Comics*
no. 1 (1941)

CHAPTER
2

That Wonder Woman is the longest-surviving and most well-known superheroine is an inarguable fact. But she was not the first major superheroine. That title belongs to two different catwomen who first appeared within four months of each other: Miss Fury and Black Cat.

Miss Fury, the very first major costumed heroine in comics, made her first appearance on the comics pages of national newspapers in April 1941 (fully eight months before the Wonder Woman's debut in *All Star* no. 1) and she lasted

until 1952. The adventures of the strip's panther skin–clad heroine were written and drawn by a woman, Tarpe Mills. Although there have been a great many women creators in the history of comics, they have rarely produced super-heroines, but Mills had been drawing action comics and costumed heroes with names like the Purple Zombie, Daredevil Barry Finn, and the Cat Man since 1938. In fact, Mills had changed her first name from June to the more sexually ambiguous Tarpe because, as she said in a 1940s

18. An advertisement for Tarpe Mills's *The Ivy Menace,* which appeared in *Amazing Man Comics* from Centaur Publications, the small publisher in whose books most of Mills's early work appeared. (*Circa* late 1930s.)

19. Tarpe Mills, creator of Miss Fury, the first major costumed superheroine, began her career in comic books, drawing action stories and costumed heroes with names like the Purple Zombie, the Cat Man, and Daredevil Barry Finn. (*Amazing Mystery Funnies* v. 2, no. 6 [whole no. 10], June 1939.)

20. Tarpe Mills, like her comic strip heroine Miss Fury, was an elegant and beautiful woman who received a great deal of attention from the press at the height of her career. Mills owned a white Persian cat named Perri-Purr, and drew her into the strip as the pet of Miss Fury's alter ego, socialite Marla Drake. Mills made newspaper headlines in 1945 when she gave Perri-Purr to the crew of an allied warship to serve as its mascot. (Photograph taken *circa* 1945.)

newspaper interview, "It would have been a major letdown to the kids if they found out that the author of such virile and awesome characters was a gal." Three years spent drawing comic book superheroes sharpened her rendering and storytelling skills so that from the beginning, Miss Fury was a stylishly drawn strip with a complicated and exciting film noir story line.

Miss Fury was Marla Drake, a beautiful socialite who bore an amazing resemblance to Mills herself. In the first episode of the comic strip, Marla discovers that another woman is planning to wear a costume identical to the one she has chosen to a masquerade ball. She rips off her costume and, at the suggestion of her French maid, dons a panther skin brought back from Africa by her explorer uncle. The skin, which fits her like a glove, supposedly belonged to a witch doctor, and carries a curse with it. In Marla's case, the curse immediately propels her into a series of adventures that take her to Brazil and pit her against Nazis, beautiful adventuresses, fiery female resistance leaders, and mad scientists.

It was hard to tell any but the simplest story in the six to eight pages usually allotted to costumed characters in the early comic books, but

21. Tarpe Mills's *Miss Fury* combined intelligently written mysteries with cinematic action sequences shown from multiple viewpoints, as demonstrated in this excerpt from the character's origin story. (Tarpe Mills, *Miss Fury*, Archival Press, 1979 [1942].)

22. Miss Fury's archenemy was the blonde Baroness Elsa Von Kampf, an international adventuress who stole Marla Drake's fiancé, Gary Hale. (*Miss Fury*, 1941.)

because *Miss Fury* ran in the pages of newspapers, the stories could be much longer and more complicated. Actually, the stories never really ended; one adventure simply segued into the next. One continuous adventure lasted the duration of World War II. Marla was never sent to the front, but found plenty of action and exotic adventure fighting Nazis in Brazil, constantly finding herself in and out of costume and in and out of captivity. Her major nemesis was the one-armed General Bruno, who commanded a battalion of Nazi soldiers hidden in the hollowed-out interior of a Brazilian mountain. At times she switched captors and became the prisoner of Era, a fiery Carmen Miranda look-alike leader of a band of anti-Nazi guerrillas, while at other times both she and Era were prisoners of the Nazis.

Further intrigue was added to the strip when Miss Fury had to contend with her beautiful and ruthless archenemy, the platinum blonde Baroness Elsa Von Kampf. The baroness was not a committed Nazi, but an amoral adventuress who had stolen Marla's boyfriend and was happy to give her allegiance to whomever had the money. Then there were the love interests: Gary Hale, Marla's handsome but weak fiancé; white-haired detective Dan Carey, who secretly loved her; "Fingers" Martin, a small time Brooklyn crook with a heart of gold; and Albino Jo, the

Harvard-educated albino Indian, also known as "the man with tiger eyes."

By the end of the war, Marla had rescued a beautiful two-year-old boy from the mad scientist Doctor Diman, who had planned to use the child in his evil experiments. She adopts the child, never knowing he is a product of the annulled marriage of Baroness Von Kampf and Gary Hale, abandoned by the unscrupulous baroness. As for the platinum-haired German bombshell, she is dragged, kicking and screaming, into a car driven by a German officer whom she had betrayed, only to surface again, with another hairdo, as a shady lady in 1947. Marla returns home with her adopted son and is promptly kidnapped, and a double substituted in her place. Only Marla's white Persian cat, Perri-Purr, is aware that the woman who claims to be Marla Drake is actually an impostor.

Tarpe Mills actually had a white Persian cat named Perri-Purr, and made newspaper headlines in 1945 when she donated the cat to the war effort. The *Miami Daily News* story, headlined "Cartoon Strip Cat Goes Off To War" and subtitled "It's Sir Admiral Purr Now," told how her cat had joined the crew of an allied warship as its mascot. The article described Perri-Purr: "He's as formidable-looking in real life as in the comic strip and the vessel's commander predicted that if he once condensed to rat-killing, he'd clean out the ship in a hurry."

If Tarpe Mills's life was not quite as glamorous as her comic strip counterpart (and it is doubtful that she would have really wanted to be captured by Nazis!), she was nevertheless in the public eye. Many newspaper articles were written about the beautiful comic creator and her alter ego heroine. According to press releases supplied by the Bell Syndicate during the war, a large naval training unit voted Miss Fury their favorite of America's comics page heroines, and a poll taken in American offices showed one hundred percent of the men and ninety percent of the women to be fans of the panther skin–wearing heroine. In 1943, even *Time* magazine got into the act, with an article that likened General Bruno to "mysterious general Gunther Niedenfuhr . . . military attaché in Brazil."

Mills's strips were eventually reprinted in comic book form. The *Miss Fury* comic book ran for eight issues and sold more than a million

23. When Marla Drake transformed herself into Miss Fury, she wore a form-fitting costume made from the skin of a black panther, a ceremonial robe brought back from Africa by her explorer uncle. (Top: *Miss Fury,* 1942; bottom: *Miss Fury,* 1946.)

24. Linda Turner was an actress who was inspired to become the Black Cat, foe of criminals and fifth columnists when, in this origin story, she suspected her director of being a Nazi spy. This first story was written by Alfred Harvey (1913–1994) and drawn by Al Gabriele. (*Pocket Comics* no. 1, 1941; reprinted in *The Original Black Cat* no. 6, August 1991.)

25. The Black Cat was rendered in the elegant and expressionistic brushwork of woman cartoonist Jill Elgin in stories published in *Speed Comics* before the character received her own book. (*Speed Comics,* pre-1946.)

copies. Had it not been for the wartime paper shortage, which limited the amount of paper available to publishers, the books would have had an even greater circulation.

Miss Fury was the first costumed heroine in newspaper strips. Four months later, the first major costumed heroine in comic books was introduced to the American public in the pages of *Pocket Comics* no. 1, a mini-sized comic book published by Alfred Harvey. "Linda Turner, Hollywood movie star, and America's sweetheart, is bored with her ultra-sophisticated life of make believe," explained the opening caption to *The Black Cat.* "She becomes the *Black Cat*—

her most adventurous role—and pledges to expose fifth columnists."

In her origin story, written by Harvey and drawn by Al Gabriele, the red-haired actress, whose name was obviously inspired by forties screen star Lana Turner, suspects her director of being a Nazi spy. Using the same logic that inspired Batman to dress up as a bat—because "criminals are a superstitious and cowardly lot"—she dons a harlequin mask and appropriate costume upon discovering that her director fears black cats. Meanwhile, ace reporter Rick Horne is also trying to "get the dope on that Nazi spy ring," and the two wind up working together to

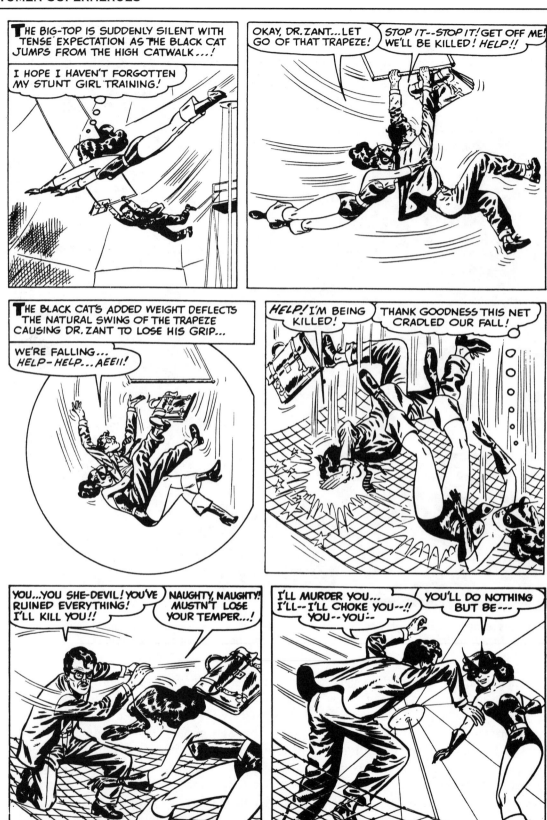

26. Linda Turner, aka The Black Cat, began her Hollywood career as a stunt woman, and shows off her skills in these panels by Lee Elias (b. 1920) from a story called, "The Circus Vandals." Elias became the regular Black Cat artist when the character got her own book in 1946. (Reprinted in *Recollections Sampler* no. 1, 1991.)

27. Leopold "Lee" Elias, was an English-born comic artist, commercial illustrator, and painter who worked for all the major U.S. comic book companies. He began his comic book career at Fiction House; his work on *Firehair, Queen of the Sagebrush Frontier* (whose scripts were always attributed to the Fiction House pen name John Starr) served as a prelude to his becoming the regular Black Cat artist. (*Rangers Comics* no. 18, April 1946.)

every story shows the clueless reporter telling Linda "what a gal" the Black Cat is, while her silent film star father, the only person to know her real identity, winks knowingly at the reader.

Pocket Comics lasted for three issues, then Black Cat moved to *Speed Comics* where she continued to be drawn by Al Gabriele and other artists, including Bob Powell, Arthur Cazeneuve, Pierce Rice, and woman cartoonist Jill Elgin. Finally, in 1946 she got her own book and a permanent artist, Lee Elias, who created the definitive Black Cat. Elias, whose polished style and bold, sure brushstrokes were inspired by Milton Caniff's *Terry and the Pirates,* drew well-defined and realistic women characters. A year before, he had become the regular artist on *Firehair,* a Western comic with another strong and beautiful female protagonist. Firehair, a white woman brought up by Indians, fought varmints such as white cattle rustlers and crooked government men intent on stealing her adopted tribes' land.

The war ended, Black Cat was no longer fighting Axis spies, and her introductory paragraph was altered to read: "Linda Turner, Hollywood star and America's sweetheart, becomes bored with her ultra-sophisticated life of movie make-believe and takes to crime-fighting in her most dramatic role of

28. Alfred Harvey (left), founder and publisher of Harvey Comics as well as the author of many Harvey scripts and the creator of the Black Cat, with Black Cat artist Lee Elias (right) in the Harvey Comics offices in New York. (Photograph, mid-1940s.)

bring the spies to justice. In the last panel, Rick sits at his desk, saying, "The Black Cat! What a gal! I'll find out who she is next time—"

But Rick is never to find out. Although he becomes Linda Turner's constant companion, his heart belongs to Black Cat, and he somehow never connects the two women. The last panel of

all as the—*Black Cat.*" Fittingly, Elias's deft use of heavy shadows in *Black Cat* created a film noir world on the comics pages, somewhat similar to that of Miss Fury. Once she had her own book the feline heroine could star in longer, more sophisticated stories. Because of her alter ego's profession, they often had film or entertainment themes.

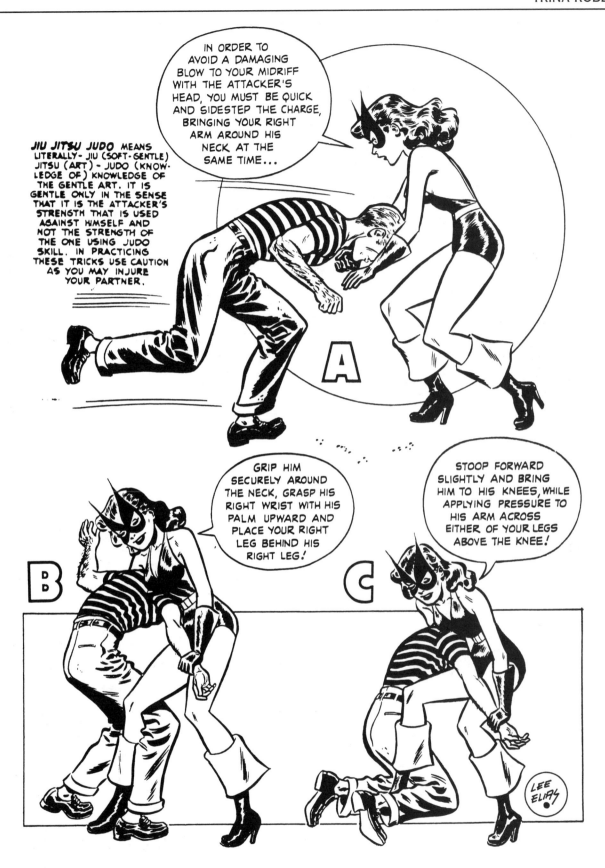

29. In keeping with the realism of the *Black Cat* stories, which were always logically structured and without magical or supernatural elements, the comic books featured convincing demonstrations of judo techniques drawn by Lee Elias. (*Black Cat Comics*, mid-1940s; reprinted in *The Original Black Cat* no. 3, 1990.)

30. Cats have provided the inspiration for a number of male and female costumed heroes, including a short-lived feature, *Cat-Man*, drawn by Tarpe Mills in *Amazing Man Comics*, nos. 5 and 8. Better known is the Cat-Man created for Holyoke Publications by Charles Quinlan, who acquired a female sidekick, the Kitten, aka Katie Conn, a trained acrobat whose parents had been killed in a train wreck. (Advertisement from the early 1940s.)

Because Linda Turner had started in films as a stunt girl, the stories also provided many opportunities to demonstrate her athletic and acrobatic skills.

Unlike the fantasy-laden *Wonder Woman,* *Black Cat* was a comic set very much in the real world. The stories were logical, and structured in a satisfyingly straightforward fashion. Supernatural elements were always debunked, and there was a rational reason for everything. It wasn't unusual for her to swing from ropes or leap from balconies onto the backs of evildoers, bringing her skills as a stuntwoman to her new career as a crime fighter. She traveled through the city streets astride a motorcycle, used a portable phone, and her preferred fighting mode was judo. Issues of *Black Cat* drawn by Lee Elias included pages in which the superheroine was depicted demonstrating various judo tricks. In all cases, Black Cat was seen defending herself against an assailant, and genuine judo techniques were shown. These were drawn and explained so clearly that a reader could conceivably learn something about judo from the pages.

With issue no. 16, the comic book, inspired by the rising popularity of western films, became *Black Cat Western,* and Linda Turner, as the new introductory paragraph reads, "turns to Western thrillers for added excitement, still keeping her identity secret in her most dramatic role as the crime fighting *Black Cat.*" The adventures in the new sagebrush setting were just as fast-paced as those set in Hollywood, but the heroine switched her mode of transportation from well-drawn motorcycles to equally well-drawn horses. Plainly, there was nothing Lee Elias couldn't draw.

The comic book remained a Western for only four issues. In 1951, with issue no. 29, it became *Black Cat Mystery,* although it briefly returned to the Western format for issues no. 54, 55 and 56. In all of its incarnations, *Black Cat* lasted until issue no. 65, coming to an end in 1963. Black Cat had survived for twenty-two years, seventeen of them in her own book. She was the second longest-lived woman superhero in comic books, and the most believable.

Miss Fury and Black Cat were the first cat heroines in comics, but they were not the last. In fact, a veritable menagerie of animal, bird, and insect women have graced the pages of comic books and continue to do so. Some were merely girlfriends or sidekicks of the various male animal heroes, such as Hawkgirl, Owlgirl, and Kitten, but many more stood—or flew—on their own.

Aside from cats, the nonhuman creature most often identified with women seems to have been the spider. This association probably predates even the ancient Greek myth of Arachne, the weaver who boasted that her talent surpassed Hera, and so was turned into a spider by the angry goddess. Comic books have been positively crawling with spider heroines, starting with Spider Queen in 1941.

The Spider Queen, who appeared in *Eagle* comics, possessed a trait that would be used twenty years later by the Marvel comics superhero, Spider-Man: spider webbing, which she wore around her wrists in specially designed bracelets and used, as the future superhero would, to swing from high place to high place. But the Spider Queen was never bitten by any radioactive spider. Her first adventure asks the question, "Just who is the Spider Queen?," and answers it: "Only two years ago she was plain Shannon Kane! Wife and assistant to a brilliant young government chemist, on a special assignment!" But Shannon's husband was killed by "enemies of his country" and Shannon took over his laboratory saying, "So Harry's gone—and I'll have to carry on somehow!" In her husband's files, she found a formula for "spider-web fluid." Experimenting with it, she discovered that "it sticks like glue—and it's actually strong enough to swing on!" She designed the special spider webbing bracelets, and became "The Spider Queen! Sworn enemy of saboteurs, racketeers, gangsters—criminals of every sort!" Although the adventures of Shannon, alias the Spider Queen, were credited to "Elsa Lesau," it appears that this was a pseudonym used by two male creators. The stories were probably the work of two brothers who collaborated on the artwork for the comic. Louis and Arturo Cazeneuve worked closely together, with Arturo inking over his brother's penciled art. Why they would have used a feminine pseudonym in a field in which women felt that they had to use male pseudonyms is a mystery.

Obviously, the Spider Queen got her name because of the spider webbing she used. It's not so easy to figure out a reason for the naming of the Spider Widow, who ran in *Feature* comics in 1942 and 1943, and was drawn by Frank M.

31. Long before Spider-Man appeared in 1962, his habit of swinging from high places using spider webbing was anticipated by the Spider Queen. Shannon Kane, widow of a brilliant young chemist killed by enemy agents, shoots her husband's "spider-web fluid" from specially designed bracelets as she pursues evildoers in stories credited to "Elsa Lesau," but probably drawn by the team of brothers Louis and Arturo Cazeneuve. (*Eagle Comics* no. 2, 1941.)

Booth. When lovely Dianne Grayton turns into the Spider Widow, she acquires a witch's face, but is attired in a long, slinky black dress. Perhaps the female spider's reputation for eating her mate was enough reason to give that name to any superheroine with a tough, don't-mess-with-me attitude. While it was common for super-heroes to have female sidekicks, the Spider Widow turned the tables by having a male side-kick named the Raven.

Another costumed heroine who bore the name of a deadly insect was the Silver Scorpion. Her adventures were published in 1941 and 1942, first in *Daring Mystery* comics, and later in *Comedy* comics. In real life, the Silver Scorpion was Betty Barstow, whose job as secretary to detective Dan Hurley put her in a good position to keep track of the criminal element. True to the traditions of comic book alter egos, Betty was the type of girl who fainted at the drop of a hat, but as soon as she was alone, she threw on a silver costume and became a caped and masked master of the arts of self-defense. Like Black Cat, she shared her fighting skills with the comics reading public. The last panel of the Silver Scorpion story published in April 1942 promised: "Boys! Girls!

The Silver Scorpion explains the Jiu Jitsu tricks she uses in the next issue."

Hawkgirl and Owlgirl, as previously noted, were merely the sidekick/girlfriends of super-heroes. But Black Canary was one bird who flew alone, even though she originated as a char-acter in someone else's comic strip. In 1947, the dashing superheroine made her first appearance in the Johnny Thunder strip, which ran in *Flash Comics*. She was a sort of female Robin Hood, working outside the law and stealing from crimi-nals. Johnny Thunder, a less interesting charac-ter whose chief talent was the ability to call on a living thunderbolt for help, retired within the year. Black Canary took his place in the comic book, fleshed out with a secret identity as brunette flower-shop owner Dinah Drake, who disguised herself in a blonde wig to fight crime. Dinah, who by the way neither sang nor flew, was given a private eye boyfriend, Larry Lance. Larry couldn't have been much of a detective, since he never guessed her true identity.

Black Canary was pretty tough. Like Black Cat, she was a master of judo and an expert motorcyclist. Her one gimmick, which she only used occasionally, was her "unique Black Canary choker." Her writer, Robert Kanigher, relied on the choker as a last resort when his superheroine was in a jam and nothing else could get her out. Unfortunately for the believability of the stories, Kanigher seemed to conveniently forget from issue to issue just what the choker could do. Depending on the needs of the plot, in one story the choker would dispense an obscuring smoke screen, while in another it contained a razor-sharp blade that enabled Black Canary to cut the ropes that bound her. Despite Carmine Infantino's excellent art, Black Canary sported

I WISH I COULD FORGET ABOUT THIS "RAVEN", WHOEVER HE IS .... YET IF IT HADN'T BEEN FOR HIM I'D BE IN A NAZI CONCENTRATION CAMP BY NOW!

With THESE THOUGHTS DIANNE GRAYTON, THE MYSTERIOUS "SPIDER WIDOW" BUSIES HERSELF ABOARD THE MIDNIGHT EXPRESS AS IT ROARS INTO THE MOUNTAIN COUNTRY OF THE EAST COAST.

32. An unusual hero was the Spider Widow, who dressed in what appeared to be a witch's mask and costume, more suitable for trick-or-treating than crime fighting: "Beneath the mask of the Spider Widow was the beautiful, athletic Dianne Grayton, society dar-ling! Unknown to all, she wages a lone crusade against the forces of evil with only the aid of her black widow spiders!" In the sto-ries, drawn by Frank Borth, she has a male sidekick called the Raven who wears wings and a helmet mask, an outfit that resembles an Aztec warrior's costume. (*Feature Comics*, 1942.)

33. The Silver Scorpion, who in real life was Betty Barstow, secretary to detective Dan Hurley, appeared in the Timely comics *Daring Mystery* and its successor, *Comedy Comics*, in 1941 and 1942. (*Comedy Comics* no. 9, 1942.)

one of the more impractical getups in comics. Dinah Drake must have spent a fortune to keep herself in tights, as her fishnet hose couldn't possibly have survived all those spectacular fights! And didn't her blonde wig ever fall off in the middle of a particularly acrobatic action scene? Nevertheless, the Black Canary lasted as long as *Flash Comics,* which was discontinued in 1949. She also appeared in *All Star Comics* as part of a superhero group, the Justice Society of America, whose members included Wonder Woman. The Justice Society, and the Black Canary, ended in 1951.

It only took six months from her first appearance in someone else's comic for Black Canary to star as a superheroine in her own story. It took Catwoman fifty years. Starting with the first issue of *Batman* comics in 1940, and for half a century thereafter, the Catwoman was one of a colorful pantheon of villains with whom Batman and Robin did battle regularly. From the beginning, however, she was different. Unlike the Joker, the Penguin, Two-Face, and the others, the pretty jewel thief never killed. In fact, she saved Batman's life several times, even risking her own

34. Dinah Drake, left, and in her secret identity as Black Canary, right. Black Canary was introduced in the Johnny Thunder strip in *Flash Comics* no. 86, and within a half-dozen issues the motorcycle-riding superheroine had replaced him. Her blonde wig, fishnet tights, and tight bolero jacket made up one of the more impractical getups in comics. (*Flash Comics* no. 95, 1948; art by Carmine Infantino and Frank Giacoia.)

35. In a 1944 issue of *Detective Comics*, Catwoman was depicted by artist Jerry Robinson wearing a cat helmet mask that covered her entire head. (*Detective Comics*, 1944; reprinted in *Batman* no. 255, March–April 1974.)

to do so. Catwoman was very much in the tradition of Milton Caniff's Dragon Lady, or the shady ladies of Will Eisner's comic strip, *The Spirit*, who harbor soft spots in their hearts for the hero and are never really bad.

"The princess of plunder," as she was sometimes called, wore a purple dress with matching boots and cat mask, and lived surrounded by cats. She had once been Selena Kyle, a stewardess, who lost her memory in a plane crash and turned to a life of crime. When she got her memory back, Selena tried to go straight and opened a small pet shop, but she resented her loss of power. In the story, "The Crimes of Catwoman," small-time crooks come into Selena's shop and harass her. She tells them, "When I was *Catwoman*, cheap crooks like you wouldn't have dared come near me!" The ultimate humiliation comes when she has to be rescued by Batman. Angrily she says, "Thanks, *Batman,* for *protecting* me! Did you come to gloat over your past victory over *Catwoman?*" Then she puts on her costume once more, announcing, "No one laughed at me when I wore *this!*" and returns to the wrong side of the law, which is where her fans liked to see her.

Through the years, though Catwoman's origin went through many changes, she remained the longest-lived and most intriguing villainess in comic books. Finally, in 1989, she became a superheroine in a mini-series written by Mindy Newell and drawn by J. J. Birch and Michael Blair.

36. Ten years later, Catwoman is still wearing a dress and rolled-top boots, but her mask has been redesigned to be much closer to that worn by Batman. (*Detective Comics* no. 211, 1954.)

Can USA rest, or
must she always
keep watch?

–from "USA, the Spirit
of Old Glory,"
Feature Comics
no. 45 (1941)

CHAPTER
3

37. USA, the Spirit of Old Glory, first appeared in *Feature Comics* no. 42, wearing a magic flag that drooped to warn of danger to the country from foreign agents and carrying a torch like that of the Statue of Liberty. (*Feature Comics*, 1941.)

onder Woman fought the Axis. So did Black Cat and Miss Fury. And the United States had not even gone to war yet! But even before Pearl Harbor this country had already taken sides in the great war that was ravaging Europe, and the country's mood was reflected in the media of the day: magazines, radio, film, and comics.

World War II was the first war in which uniformed women took an active part. Like Paradise Island in *Wonder Woman,* the home front was sometimes a country solely of women. Real-life superheroines in overalls worked round the clock in airplane and munitions plants. Wacs and Waves battled the Axis on land and sea and in the air, and so did their comic book sisters. Wearing red, white, and blue costumes that might have been designed by Betsy Ross, patriotic superheroines fought Germans and Japanese on land, on sea, in the air, and on the pages of America's comics. In their civilian life, most of them were mild-mannered secretaries or girl reporters. Many of them were drawn by women artists like Nina Albright, Jill Elgin, and Pauline Loth, who had stepped in to fill the positions left vacant when male artists went off to war.

At least six months before the United States entered the war, the Spirit of Old Glory appeared in *Feature Comics* wearing, instead of a cape, a

38. Pat Patriot, America's only singing super-heroine. Given the appellation "America's Joan of Arc," Pat proudly wore a red, white, and blue costume with a wide belt buckled with a big star. (*Daredevil Comics,* 1941.)

39. Three panels from the 1942 story drawn by Lin Streeter that featured Pat Patriot singing at a nightclub benefit for America's defense. (*Daredevil Comics,* 1942.)

magic flag which drooped in times of danger. Her name was USA, and we'll never know just how it was supposed to be pronounced. Oosa? Yoosa? She was a goddesslike flying woman who carried a torch of freedom. ("As long as the torch of freedom lights the way, our might on land and sea shall not perish.") The creators of USA played it safe; because our country was not at war yet, they didn't give the enemy a specific name. Instead, the bad guys are referred to as "aggressors," "the foreign power" and, as USA refers to them, "the pretentious enemy." But artist Maurice Gutwirth drew them to look suspiciously like Nazis.

In 1941, the writer of *Pat Patriot, America's Joan of Arc,* didn't name the enemy either. When the heroine (beautifully depicted in boots, a striped skirt, and a wide belt buckled with a big star) catches a gang who has attempted to blow up a dam, they are described as "wanted by the FBI." But a year after Pearl Harbor, in *Daredevil Comics* no. 10, the heroine, in a story drawn by Lin Streeter, stars in a nightclub benefit for government defense and sings: "Peoples of the Americas, I'm here to say . . . that hate shall never purge the earth . . . Democracy shall have its say!" German agents try to kill her because "Too much good will she is winning! Der future of Germany demands dat she be put oudt of der way!" Pat Patriot has no super powers; with the strength of her fists alone she puts the Nazis out

of commission, and actually finishes her song in the last panel: "America for the Americans and to heck with the Nazi blitzkrieg!" It doesn't rhyme, but the audience loves it. "What a show!" they shout. "Hooray for Pat!" "Colossal!" "Wow!" "Bravo, Pat!"

The writers of Miss Victory, in *Captain Fearless* no. 1, August 1941, were also cagey about exactly who their heroine was fighting. The enemy is simply called "organized bands" who are "operating against the best interests of the government," but the boss of the group is named "Mr. Axis." Joan Wayne, secretary at the Foreign Trade Committee in Washington, D.C., trades her eyeglasses for a mask and pulls on striped shorts, a cape, ballet shoes, and a top with a big star on the chest, to become Miss Victory. Like Pat Patriot, she is not gifted with any super powers, but she does a lot of leaping along with the requisite punching. The first story was crudely drawn by an anonymous artist, but the art improved over the heroine's comparatively long life span. By 1943, drawn much better by Charles M. Quinland, she had traded in the star on her chest for a big V, and the comic book's title had been changed to *Captain Aero.* Still wearing demure eyeglasses, Joan Wayne now works for the assistant secretary of commerce, and this time the enemy is referred to as "dirty Nazi dogs." True to superhero tradition, in the last panel Miss Victory is

40. The many faces of Miss Victory, one of the few red, white, and blue-garbed superheroines to survive World War II. Top, artist unknown (*Captain Fearless Comics*, 1941); middle row, Charles M. Quinlan (*Captain Aero Comics*, 1943); and Nina Albright (*Captain Aero Comics*, 1946).

41. Commandette, a crime fighter whose real name was a takeoff on that of pinup queen Betty Grable, appeared in only one of the two issues of *Star-Studded Comics*. (*Star-Studded Comics*, 1945.)

back in her civilian guise as a mild-mannered secretary, and while her unsuspecting boss reads a newspaper account of the superheroine's triumphs, she winks and makes the "V for Victory" sign at the reader.

Miss Victory was one of the rare patriotic superheroines to outlast the war. In 1946, and in a considerably shrunken costume, she was still going strong in the pages of *Captain Aero,* drawn by Nina Albright. By now she, like Wonder Woman, had her own remote-controlled plane, but her alter ego was still "demure Joan Wayne." Unfortunately, neither *Captain Aero* comics nor Miss Victory survived beyond 1946.

The patriotic superheroines didn't always fight the Axis—there was plenty of crime on the home front. Commandette ("That's me, the female commando!") appeared in only one issue of *Star Studded* comics, in 1944. She fought blackmailers, and was obviously inspired by Black Cat. Like Linda Turner, who became the feline superheroine, Commandette's secret identity was Betty Babble, probably a deliberate parody of pinup queen Betty Grable, and she, too, had been a stunt woman before becoming a movie star.

And one superheroine, Yankee Girl, not only changed costumes but assumed an entirely new secret identity. In 1945, the blonde superheroine appeared in issues no. 8 and no. 9 of *Captain Flight* comics as "a shy settlement worker" named Kitty Kelly. Two years later, when she reappeared in *Dynamic Comics,* she had become a brunette named Lauren Mason and gained the ability to fly. Although the war had been over for two years, her newer costume was of a much more patriotic design than the old one: a striped swimsuit and a star-studded cape.

Not only the costumes but the logos of these stories often changed. Pat Patriot and Miss Victory both went from comparatively plain logos to ones in which the title was decorated with stars and stripes to match their costume. Liberty Belle, subtitled "The All-American Girl," had a blue logo embellished with white stars, and wore a red bell on her blue shirt. In her secret identity as "Libby Belle Lawrence, noted woman reporter, radio commentator and world traveller," and with her blonde hair pulled back under a snappy fedora, the superheroine was a stronger and more interesting character then the usual superheroine alter ego of mild-mannered secretary. She had a unique method of being reached when trouble threatened. Only old Tom Revere, who guarded the original cracked Liberty Bell in Philadelphia, knew how to call her. He "strokes the historic liberty bell and faint vibrations are set up," which reach Libby Belle's miniature bell, "made of the same metals as the liberty bell." She exclaims, "Somewhere there's trouble—danger—and I'm needed!" Then she "loosens her wavy golden hair" and becomes "Liberty Belle, heroine of countless perilous exploits against the enemies of America."

Miss America shared her red, white and blue–striped and starry logo with many of the other patriotic superheroines. She was created by the prolific comic and science fiction writer Otto Binder, who seemed to specialize in well-written superheroines aimed at young girls. Next to William Moulton Marston, Binder was probably the most important superheroine creator in early comics, creating four different superheroines for three different comics publishers over a period of ten years.

The story of Miss America's origin was told in the second issue of her magazine. Sixteen-year-old Madeleine Joyce had been visiting her uncle's scientist friend. "During this visit, an electrical storm fills the heavens. Madeleine, trapped in a high-voltage cabinet, falls unconscious." When she awakens, she has the usual super powers, and can fly.

Although Miss America started as just one of many comic strips in *Marvel Mystery* no. 49, by 1944 the young superheroine had graduated to her own book. Editor Vincent Fago, who had worked as an animator in the Fleischer Studios before coming to comics, hired another ex-Fleischer animator, Pauline Loth, to draw Miss America. Loth designed a particularly tasteful and stylish version of the patriotic costume for her superheroine: a short-skirted, full-sleeved red dress emblazoned with a shield on her chest, matching tights, and a little red skullcap. In the tradition of the period, Madeleine Joyce disguised her true identity with a pair of

42. The two faces of Yankee Girl, who changed not only costumes but secret identities in her appearances in two different comic book titles. (Above: *Captain Flight Comics*, 1945; below: *Dynamic Comics*, 1947.)

harlequin glasses. But by 1946, she kept the glasses on even when in her superheroine guise, making her the only nearsighted superheroine in comics.

Loth had a clean, rounded, open style that girls liked, and it was clear from her first appearance that Miss America was aimed as specifically for a female market as Wonder Woman had been. The first issue of Miss America comics even featured two pages of paper dolls, something that is usually not of much interest to the average boy. That first issue also featured a subscription blank—a one-year subscription to *Miss America* cost a dollar—and Vincent Fago remembers that within two weeks they had received 20,000 subscriptions, so many that they had to replace the artwork in their file cabinets with the subscription money.

Miss America Comics, however, lasted only one issue, and in the second issue it became *Miss America Magazine,* featuring short fiction and articles aimed at girls, and comic strips including Miss America and long-lasting teenage comic heroine Patsy Walker. Patsy also was drawn by Pauline Loth, under her married name, Pauline O'Sullivan. After issue no. 5, the superheroine abandoned the magazine which continued to bear her name, and moved on to guest appearances in other superheroines' comic books, such as *Blonde Phantom* and *Sun Girl. Miss America Magazine,* still featuring Patsy Walker comics, lasted until 1957, but the superheroine herself hung up her blue cape in 1948.

Not every patriotic superheroine was American. Even before Pearl Harbor, comic book writers demonstrated America's partiality to our besieged and blitzkrieged neighbor across the sea by creating several British superheroines. Pat Parker, War Nurse, made her first appearance in

43. Liberty Belle's outfit of blouse, boots, and jodhpurs made her look more like the characters found in adventure strips than a superheroine. However, her role as a two-fisted defender of freedom was indicated by the patriotic colors of her blue shirt and magical red bell. Her secret identity was Libby Belle Lawrence, reporter and radio commentator. (*Star Spangled Comics* no. 25, 1943.)

Speed Comics, where the introductory paragraph referred to her as "John Bull's valiant War Nurse." Captain Pat Parker really is a British nurse, but she becomes a superheroine by taking off her white uniform to reveal an outfit consisting of a crop top and brief shorts with a cross on her belt, and by donning a mask also decorated with a red cross. Suddenly she is known as "War Nurse"! This leads to confusing scenes in which a general asks the war nurse if she knows the identity of War Nurse.

After eleven issues, Pat Parker joined the Girl Commandos as their leader. The strip, now called *Girl Commandos,* featured a sort of female

44. Miss America, drawn by former Fleischer Studios animator Pauline Loth and written by Otto Binder (1911–1974). Loth's clean and streamlined style emphasized the acrobatic qualities of Miss America's feats, and her open page designs with relatively few panels per page made her stories inviting to read. (*Miss America Magazine* no. 5, February 1945.)

United Nations, all from embattled countries, who fought the Axis in Nazi-occupied lands like Norway and Greece. Ellen, Pat, and Penny are British, Tanya is Russian, and Mei Ling is Chinese. Only Ellen wears a traditional nurse's uniform; the others dress in variations of their leader's shorts and crop top, though Pat alone gets to wear her mask and little cape. In later issues, the commandos changed to short-skirted uniforms, accessorized with wide belts, military hats, and high boots. Pat Parker and her Girl Commandos defied comic book tradition not

only by including an overweight girl, Ellen, as an action heroine who was just as tough as her sisters, but by the realistic, nonracist depiction of Mei Ling, the Chinese member of the group.

In their adventures, drawn by various artists including Jill Elgin, the Girl Commandos soon acquired an archenemy, Madame Intrigue, master of disguise. This "notorious Nazi agent" appears in varied personae: as a chambermaid, a blind beggar lady, a Greek fish peddler, a beautiful Greek "girl guerrilla," even a mysterious hooded Arab. Pat Parker and her multinational

45. Miss America paper dolls by Pauline Loth. Like Wonder Woman, Miss America was aimed specifically at a female market. (*Miss America Comics* no. 1, 1944.)

women fought for the freedom of enslaved nations right through to the end of the war, finally laying down their guns and uniforms when *Speed Comics* ended its long run in 1947.

The Black Angel, another British superheroine who appeared in *Airfighters Comics,* was, in real life, frail, sickly Sylvia Lawton. At least that's what her maiden aunt, Lady Lawton, thought. The old woman had no idea that her delicate niece, who fainted during air raids, was apt to sneak away from their castle home to her plane, hidden in an underground hangar, and become Black Angel, the ebony-clad aviatrix whose "name spells horror to swaggering Nazis." Covered from head to toe in shiny, skintight black, the superheroine, as drawn by John Cassone, bore more of a resemblance to the darker Miss Fury than to Wonder Woman's bright, flag-embossed sisters. Like Pat Parker and her Girl Com-

46. Unlike most of the patriotic superheroines of World War II who fought spies and fifth columnists in the United States, Pat Parker, War Nurse, was from Britain, and her solo adventures as well as her later heroics when she was one of the Girl Commandos were played out against the background of war-torn Europe. (*Speed Comics* no. 19, 1942.)

mandos, she also had a beautiful but evil Nazi archenemy, Baroness Blood. The blonde baroness, who wore jodhpurs and a swastika on her chest, and who of course affected a long cigarette holder, was an enemy air ace, the German equivalent of Black Angel. In later issues, the British superheroine acquired a male sidekick, the Black Prince. This was an unusual occurrence in comics, where it is traditionally the male who has a female sidekick.

Many of the Black Angel's adventures, like those of Pat Parker and friends, led her to enemy-occupied lands. One of the more dramatic stories takes place in occupied Paris, and involves a legend that Quasimodo, the Hunchback of Notre Dame, will return and call the French to revolt against their oppressors by ringing the bells of Notre Dame Cathedral. The Nazis, hoping to

destroy the French underground, bring in a half-mad hunchback named Malvino. When the resistance, led by the Black Angel and Black Prince, march on Notre Dame, singing the French national anthem, they are confronted by Malvino crouching above the bells, and they believe Quasimodo has returned. Malvino tells them to turn back: "Let no one come further . . . the bells are the sacred task of Quasimodo!" Black Angel, not easily daunted, tells her comrades to wait for Quasimodo to ring the bells. Then, when the bells do not ring, she adds, "All right! I'll ring them myself!" She and Black Prince are outnumbered by the Nazis, who tie them to the clapper of the great bell. "Now, I ring the bells," boasts the Nazi commander, "and your bodies will be crushed!!" He chortles, "It iss clever! Quieting the bells of freedom with human mutes!"

47. Pat Parker, War Nurse, and her Girl Commandos, a multinational force of women that fought the Axis in occupied Europe. Art by Jill Elgin. (*Speed Comics*, reprinted in *War Heroes Classics* no. 1, June 1991.)

48. The Black Angel, in real life the apparently frail and sickly Sylvia Lawton who pretended to quiver and faint during Nazi bombing raids of her native Britain, and her archenemy, the Baroness Blood, were both women pilots who engaged in aerial battles over Britain and France. Art by John Cassone. (*Air Fighters Comics*, vol. 1, no. 2, November 1942; reprinted in *Airfighters Classics* vol. 1, no. 1, November 1987.)

CONTACT COMICS

BLACK VENUS

BLACK VENUS IS ABOUT TO TAKE OFF ON ONE OF HER MOST DARING AND IMPORTANT ADVENTURES. AWARE OF CERTAIN DANGERS THAT CONFRONT HER, SHE HAS YET TO LEARN OF THE GREAT PERIL THAT AWAITS, LURKING IN THE SHADOWS OF THE JAP-INFESTED ISLAND WHERE HER MISSION TAKES HER.

49. In real life, Black Venus was physical therapist Mary Roche. During the war, she was a woman pilot, the American equivalent of the British Black Angel. In World War II, the only women pilots to see combat were in the comics, while real women pilots were limited to ferrying planes from factories or between airfields. After the war, stories showed medical professional Mary working with veterans who had been injured in the service. Drawn by Nina Albright. (*Contact Comics*, 1945.)

50. Madame Strange, an "American girl reporter" whose nemesis, the Octopus, was among the most bizarre caricatures of the Japanese to appear in World War–era comics. Art by Silang Isip, script by Jean Press. (Great Comics no. 3, January 1942.)

But poor mad Malvino, believing he is Quasimodo and that Black Angel is his beloved Esmeralda, sacrifices his life to save them. The caption reads, "With his last ounce of energy, the hunchback frees the two victims . . ." The people of the French underground shout, "The bells of Notre Dame!! They ring!!" "Arise, men of France!! It's freedom's song!!"

The last panel shows Black Angel's plane flying over the rooftops of Paris. Bold letters in the sky spell out "Long live France," and the caption beneath the panel reads, "There's a price on her head, but the Nazi who collects it must understand a whistling knife, a bullet aimed at the heart . . ."

Like her many costumed sisters, Black Angel only lasted as long as the comic book she was in, and both she and *Air Fighters Comics* ended, along with the war, in 1945.

Black Venus was the American equivalent of Black Angel, an aviatrix dressed in black from head to toe. Only Air Force Captain Owens knew her secret identity as Mary La Roche. Nina Albright drew her with appealing wide eyes and a spunky expression, and she fought the Axis in *Contact Comics* for two years, from 1944 until 1946.

The most abnormal of World War II's dark superheroines, aptly named Madame Strange,

appeared in *Great Comics* for their entire three-issue run during 1941 and 1942. Her story was credited to Silang Isip and Jean Press. Madame Strange wears jodhpurs and carries a riding crop. Her high, curving collar suggests Asian clothing, or possibly futuristic science fiction garb. In her other identity, she is "an American girl reporter," although even in this identity she still seems to be known as Madame Strange. But it is the villains who prove themselves to be oddest of all. Even in an industry and at a time when it was accepted practice to depict the enemy as hideous and deformed, the strip's artist outdid himself with a Japanese leader named the Octopus and his monstrous hunchbacked followers.

The Octopus was a racist's nightmare vision of the "yellow peril," with fangs and perfectly round eyes staring out of goggles. One hand was tipped in talonlike fingernails and, in place of the other hand, he had a steel claw. As with other archenemies, it was never clear at the end of each adventure whether or not the Octopus has been permanently dispatched. The reader was kept guessing and, hopefully, would buy the next issue of the comic book in order to find out.

In the last panel of one of her adventures, the heroine in her guise as girl reporter reads about her own exploits in the newspaper, while the paperboy says, "Yep lady! Uncle Sam scored again!" The caption below the panel asks, "*Did* the *Octopus* escape from a watery grave? Madame Strange finds out in the next issue of *Great Comics.*"

With the exception of Miss America, none of these superheroines had their own titles. Some didn't last for more than one issue and hardly any survived the war, often because the books they ran in didn't survive the war, either. And some were downright silly, although no more so than their male equivalents. But for four glorious years, young girls could open a comic book and read that it was possible for women, too, to help defeat fascism.

It's Linda! I hear Linda calling me! She's in danger!

*–The Flame,
Wonderworld Comics
no. 33 (1942)*

CHAPTER
4

In general, the sidekick girlfriends of the superheroes were a pain in the neck. Either their powers were weaker than those of the men, or they were just plain incompetent, for they often seemed to need rescuing. A 1952 cover of *Doll Man* no. 38 is typical. Doll Girl, tied to a stick of wood in a fireplace grate, is being menaced by a bearded, knife-wielding giant. Doll Man, billed as "the world's mightiest mite," rushes to the rescue, brandishing a burning torch. In a Rocketman story from *Punch Comics,* Rocketgirl gets shot in the back on page three, and for the rest of the story lies near death in a hospital while Rocketman searches the country for a donor who matches her rare blood type. Flame Girl, who can burst into flame like the Human Torch, gets

sidekick retained her name of Lois, even when in superheroine costume.

In *Detective Comics* no. 233, Batman acquired a woman sidekick when his girlfriend, Kathy Kane, decided to dress up in a skintight yellow costume as Batwoman, complete with motorcycle and a utility case which contained such items as sneezing powder puffs and a smoke bomb lipstick. But over one hundred issues later, in *Detective* no. 359, his new female sidekick, librarian Barbara Gordon, was given the more traditional name of Batgirl.

Sometimes the superduos were more evenly matched. Boomerang and Diana, who were drawn by L. B. Cole in the short-lived *Terrific Comics* in 1944, were both specialists in their own way. Diana, like her goddess namesake, was a whiz at the bow and arrow, and Boomerang was, of course, master of the boomerang. Also equally matched, and one of the cutest superheroine sidekicks in comics, was Super Ann Star, known as the World's Strongest Girl. She appeared with Mighty Man in a comic strip called *Mighty Man and the World's Strongest Girl,* which ran in both *Stars and Stripes* and *Amazing Man Comics* in 1941. The strip was drawn

51. The most popular superheroine of the 1940s was Mary Marvel, the only female member of Fawcett Publications' Marvel Family of characters. The Marvels gained their super powers by uttering the word "Shazam," which invoked the magical forces of classical gods and goddesses.

extinguished when she is doused with water in a mine tunnel. The Flame has to come to her rescue. In the last panel of this 1942 story from *Wonderworld Comics,* he stands at her hospital bed, saying, "Thank heavens, *Linda,* the doctor says your *sight* will be *saved,* but you must promise *never* to use your *flame power* again! You are not strong enough to *control* it, and I could *never* bear to *lose* you!"

Even their names told the reader who was the stronger and who was the weaker of the pair. Bulletman, Doll Man, Rocketman, Hawkman, the Owl and the Flame had as their female counterparts Bulletgirl, Doll Girl, Hawkgirl, Owlgirl and Flame Girl. There was literally not a woman among them. Perhaps because "Bolt Girl" sounded too awkward, Blue Bolt's girlfriend-

by Martin Filchock in a disarmingly simple style, and Mighty Man himself was a rather interesting character. In the introductory splash panel, we are told that "he can grow . . . he can shrink" and "He can change his features." Although she doesn't possess Mighty Man's unique talents, Super Ann, depicted as always running on her tiptoes, ballerina-style, has powers that are closer to those of Superman. She is shown racing a speeding locomotive and leaping tall buildings at a single bound. She pushes trains and trucks to a stop, bends steel as though it were butter, and tosses rocks as though they were pebbles. The reader never learns if bullets bounce off her. The explanation for her super powers? "An old man from another planet taught her how to perform those feats of strength"!

52. A sidekick in peril. Doll Man, created by Will Eisner (b. 1917) for Quality Comics, first appeared in *Feature Comics* in 1939, but received a female counterpart only when the character's popularity began to fade. Martha Roberts, the fiancée of Doll Man Darrel Dane, joined the hero in *Doll Man* no. 37, December 1951, but the comic lasted only ten more issues, folding in 1953. (*Dollman* no. 38, 1952.)

a. LINDA DALE IS TRANSFORMED INTO THE FLAME GIRL!

b. IN THE *MIDWAY CITY MUSEUM* OFFICE WHERE THE PUBLIC KNOWS THEM AS *CARTER HALL,* CURATOR, AND HIS WIFE *SHIERA, HAWKMAN* AND *HAWKGIRL* PREPARE FOR THEIR NIGHT'S TASK ...

OF COURSE, WHAT I SAID ABOUT *CAGLIOSTRO'S* MIRROR WAS SHEER NONSENSE!

YOU KNOW THAT -- BUT THE EMERALD-THIEF *DOESN'T!*

c. ... *CHANGING PEGGY SHANE* INTO ... *GOLDEN GIRL!*

WHAT HAPPENED ??? I'M *FLYING!* WHY ... WHY, THE GOLDEN HEART CHANGED ME INTO ... *GOLDEN GIRL!*

d. —ROCKETGIRL™

e. ONLY LITTLE ME!

LOIS? BUT...

53. A gallery of "girl" sidekicks.

a. Flame Girl was the short-lived partner of Flame, Fox Features Syndicate's imitation of the Human Torch; her fire was put out when she was doused with water in a mine tunnel. (*Wonderworld Comics,* 1942.)

b. Hawkgirl, who joined Hawkman in *Flash* no. 24, never seemed to fly quite as high as her partner, but the pair have enjoyed surprising longevity, continuing to appear until the end of the runs of the golden-age *Flash* and *All Star Comics* in 1949 and 1951, and enjoying revivals in a variety of DC titles up to the present day (including two series of *Hawkman Comics,* 1964–1968 and 1986–1987).

c. Like other golden-age girl sidekicks, Golden Girl joined Captain America only when the patriotic character was losing readers as his appeal faded with the end of World War II. In *Captain America Comics* no. 66, the hero revealed his secret identity to Betsy Ross, who became his new companion, replacing his injured sidekick, Bucky. (*Captain America Comics.*)

d. Rocketgirl was unusual in originating simultaneously with Rocketman in *Punch Comics* no. 9, rather than as a circulation-building afterthought, but like other women sidekicks she often needed rescuing. (*Punch Comics.*)

e. Blue Bolt, famous for being the first character that saw the team-up of comic book giants Joe Simon (b. 1915) and Jack Kirby (1917–1994), was Fred Parrish, a football player struck by lightning and given super powers thanks to radium treatments. His girl-friend, Lois Blake, got a similar costume and powers in *Blue Bolt* vol. 2, no. 7, but perhaps because "Bolt Girl" sounded too awkward, she was still just plain Lois even when dressed to fight crime. (*Blue Bolt.*)

f. Newspaper reporter Belle Wayne was the fiancee of detective Nick Terry, and joined him as Owl Girl in February 1941 after discovering his secret identity as the Owl. (*Crackajack Funnies.*)

g. Bullet Girl joined Bulletman when the Fawcett character received his own book in 1941. (*Bulletman.*)

OH, BATMAN--I'M AFRAID YOU'LL JUST HAVE TO HOLD ME! I'M STILL SHAKY AFTER FIGHTING CLAYFACE-- AND YOU'RE SO STRON-NN-G!

54. Batman's female sidekicks have included Kathy Kane, who became Batwoman in *Detective Comics* no. 233 (July 1956); her blonde niece, Betty, who became Bat-Girl in *Batman* no. 139 (April 1961); and Barbara Gordon, who became Batgirl in *Detective Comics* no. 359 (January 1967). The coy Bat-Girl above was drawn by golden-age veteran Sheldon Moldoff. (*Batman* no. 159, November 1963.)

Sometimes the female sidekicks were relatives rather than girlfriends of the superheroes. Catman, who had his own comic book from 1941 through 1946, fought crime alongside his niece, Katie. Charles Quinlan drew her in pigtails, looking about thirteen years old. When she put on a mask and cat suit which was an exact replica of that worn by her uncle David, and became the Kitten, she was brave and resourceful enough to rescue him from his Nazi captors.

Merry, the Girl of a Thousand Gimmicks, was the younger sister of the Star Spangled Kid, a superhero who started in *Star Spangled Comics* no. 1. She first appeared in issue no. 81, a cute red-haired teenager with a mask and a red, white and blue costume, written by the amazing Otto Binder, who seemed to specialize in superheroines. Armed with no super powers, but a mile-high attitude and a pocket full of gimmicks—bulletproof catcher's mitts, squirt-guns, firecrackers, and more—she outlasted her brother and continued to star in lighthearted adventure stories until the comic book ceased publication in 1952.

By far the best sister in comics was Captain Marvel's twin, Mary Marvel. Marc Swayze, who designed Mary and drew her first three adventures, remembers that the idea of a long-lost

sister to the white-caped superhero came from "upstairs" at Fawcett Publications, probably cooked up between editorial director Ralph Daigh and comics editor Ed Herron. When editor Rod Reed approached Swayze with the idea in 1942 and asked him for some character sketches, his first sketch was okayed immediately and Mary Marvel was born.

In Mary's origin story in Captain Marvel Adventures no. 18, she learns that Billy Batson is her brother, and that the two had been separated at birth. She correctly surmises that the magic word "Shazam" will transform her just as it does her brother, and after the thunderclouds clear away, she stands revealed in a short-skirted version of Captain Marvel's red costume, as Mary Marvel, the World's Mightiest Girl. When little Billy says the magic word, he becomes the adult Captain Marvel, while Mary, in true sidekick tradition, stays young. Because Mary was never any older than fourteen, it was easy for young female readers to relate to her. She was a girl like them, and if she could become a superheroine, perhaps they could, too. One wonders how many young girls, in the years between 1942 and 1954, experimentally whispered or shouted "Shazam!" in the privacy of their bedrooms, to no avail.

The meanings behind the letters in Shazam varied depending on who uttered the word. When spoken by Billy, they stood for Solomon, Hercules, Atlas, Zeus, Achilles, and Mercury. But in Mary's case they meant Selena, Hippolyta, Ariadne, Zephyrus, Aurora, and Minerva. No one who read the comic seemed either to know or care that Zephyrus was a male deity to whom the comic's creators had given a sex change; the god was always drawn in the comic as a female.

Mary could fly, and she was every bit as invulnerable as her brother; bullets bounced off her. Marc Swayze designed her with curly, shoulder-length brown hair as a girl-next-door type no older than twelve or thirteen. When he went into the service, various other artists drew the teenaged superheroine and aged her by a year or two. Later, Swayze drew a newspaper strip about an aviatrix, Flyin' Jenny, delineating the adventure heroine with the same dashing style he had given to the flying teenager.

Artists who took over Mary Marvel after Swayze included Kurt Shaffenberger, Captain Marvel creator C. C. Beck and, most importantly,

GIANT BATMAN

55. Batgirl gets dressed, from a late 1960s story in which she was described in Gardner Fox's script as the "dominoed dare-doll" and the "chic crime-fighter!" Art by Carmine Infantino and Sid Green. (Originally published 1967, reprinted in *Batman* no. 255, March–April 1974.)

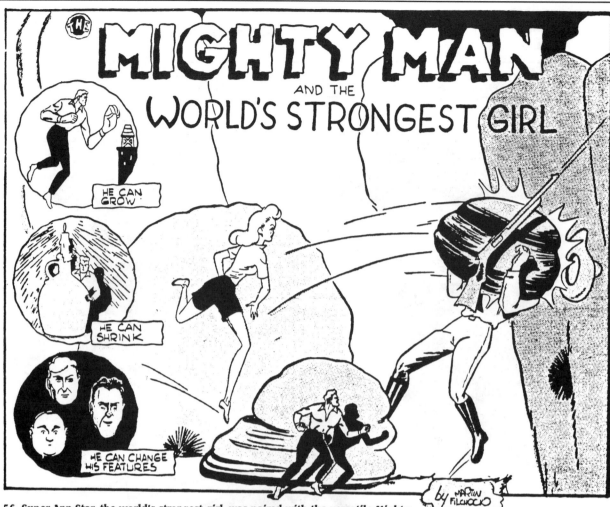

56. Super Ann Star, the world's strongest girl, was paired with the versatile Mighty Man in Centaur's *Amazing Man* and *Stars and Stripes* comics. (*Amazing Man*, 1941.)

57. Super Ann in action. Drawn by prolific editorial and gag cartoonist Martin Filchock in a disarmingly simple style, she was dressed like a woman athlete, posed like a ballerina and, like Superman, was faster than a speeding bullet and able to leap tall buildings in a single bound. (*Amazing Man*, 1941.)

Jack Binder, whose brother Otto wrote Mary's adventures. Of the many costumed heroines written by Otto Binder, this teenager, in her red dress emblazoned with a lightning bolt, must have held a special place in his heart. Around five years after her creation, he and his wife Ione adopted a baby girl and named her Mary, after his young superheroine.

Like Wonder Woman, many of Mary Marvel's adventures included a strong fantasy element. At various times her stories featured gnomes, witches, mummies, and beautiful princesses. Obviously aware of who comprised their readership, Mary Marvel's writers also often dealt with girls' special problems. In a 1945 issue of *Wow Comics,* Mary tackled the age-old headache of the boys' club. When Mary Batson and her girlfriends try to join the "Boys Fun Club," they are told, "Scram, we don't want any silly old girls in our club!" Mary suggests, "Why can't we have *our own girls club?*" The girls pick an old abandoned house for their new clubhouse: "We can fix it up nifty!" But inside they find crates full of stolen goods. "Crooks have been using this old deserted house to hide their loot!" exclaims Mary. As Mary Marvel, she helps her friends catch the crooks and hand them over to the police. Then the boys arrive, having had a change of heart. "Say," says one. "We—uh—heard how you girls licked those crooks! We—uh—thought maybe you would like to join our club now!" But the girls are no longer interested in joining the boys' club. One girl tells them, "We've decided to have our own club now—the *Mary Marvel club!* It's in honor of Mary Marvel, the Shazam girl!"

And indeed, on the last page, readers are invited to join the Mary Marvel club for ten cents (in coin or stamps). Mary herself promises them that "members will receive a membership card, a magic badge, plus a letter from me every now and then in which I'll try to cover topics which will be of interest to you." Any magic badges that may still be in existence are sure to be worth quite a bit more than ten cents today.

Girls who really wanted to emulate their heroine could even buy Mary Marvel fashions. A 1947 advertisement in comic strip form that ran in *Wow Comics* was titled "Mary Marvel Copies a Cowboy." The shorts, dungarees, and plaid shirt that could be ordered through the mail came in girls' sizes seven to fourteen, and the most expensive item of clothing cost $3.95.

58. Merry, the Girl of a Thousand Gimmicks, was the younger sister of the Star Spangled Kid, a superhero teenager with an adult sidekick who was created by Jerry Siegel, the creator of Superman. Her origin and many of her subsequent adventures were scripted by Otto Binder, who seemed to have a special feel for superheroines, and she quickly replaced her older brother in *Star Spangled Comics.* (*Star Spangled Comics,* late 1940s.)

The CAT-MAN and the **KITTEN**

by CHAS. M. QUINLAN

59. The Cat-Man was David Merrywether, who acquired catlike abilities when he was reared by a tigress after his family was killed by bandits in Burma. When he returned to the United States and became a costumed super-hero, he recruited another orphan to be his sidekick and Katie Conn became the Kitten, who often called Cat-Man "Uncle David." (*Cat-Man* no. 12, 1942.)

60. When the editors at Fawcett came up with the idea of creating a sister for Fawcett's wildly successful Captain Marvel, artist Marcus Desha "Marc" Swayze (b. 1920) was asked to prepare concepts for the character's design. This, his first sketch, was approved immediately, and Mary Marvel's origin appeared in *Captain Marvel Adventures* no. 18, December 1942. The image of Mary's head at left is not by Swayze; it is a stat pasted on the sketch at a later date. (Pencil sketch on paper, 1942; collection of Mark Swayze.)

GOOD HEAVENS! IS IT SOME GHOST-- OR SPIRIT---OR WHAT? BUT NO TIME TO WASTE----

SHAZAM!

WHEN MARY BATSON UTTERS THE NAME OF THE ANCIENT WIZARD, MAGIC LIGHTNING CRASH-ES DOWN WHICH GIVES HER ALL THE POWERS OF SIX GREAT GODDES-SES ROLLED INTO THE FORM OF-- MARY MARVEL!

BOOM!

THE SHAZAM GIRL ATTACKS THE MYSTERIOUS BEING!

IF YOU'RE A GHOST, YOU HAVE A MIGHTY SOLID CHIN!

UGG!

WHACK

61. Mary Marvel was the long-lost sister of newsboy Billy Batson, who could transform himself into the adult hero, Captain Marvel, by uttering the magic word "Shazam!" Unlike Billy, Mary remained a young girl when she became a superheroine, a graceful flying figure, and powerful fighter for good that young female readers could identify with. (*Wow Comics* no. 58, September 1947.)

I COULD NEVER PICTURE MARY BEING SHOT THROUGH THE AIR LIKE A PROJECTILE...

...SHE SHOULD FLY WITH THE GRACE OF A MEADOWLARK AND LIGHT LIKE A FEATHER!

62. Marc Swayze gave Mary Marvel her crown of chestnut ringlets and the grace and agility that made her the most genuinely athletic member of the Marvel Family. Although other artists, most notably Otto Binder's brother Jack (1902–1974), drew her adventures after her creator entered the service, they followed the pattern set by Swayze. The power and elegance of his conception is demonstrated in this recent series of sketches.

63. This public-service page from *Wow Comics* demonstrates why Mary Marvel's comic books are so expensive and hard to find today. During World War II, most of them, along with most other comic books, were routinely recycled for the war effort. (*Wow Comics* no. 39, November–December 1945.)

64. Below: A gathering of some of the key personnel of Fawcett Publications in their offices in New York in 1942. Left to right: Mercedes Schull, editor of *Wow Comics;* editor Tom Naughton; writer and editor Otto Binder, who wrote Mary Marvel's origin story and more than half the scripts for Captain Marvel and the other members of the Marvel Family; editor and writer John Beardsley, and executive editor Rod Reed, with pipe.

65. Overleaf: In 1939, Russell Keaton (1909–1945), the artist who had ghosted the finest *Buck Rogers* Sunday pages for Dick Calkins, began his own strip, *Flyin' Jenny,* the first and only comic strip about a woman aviator, and engaged Marc Swayze as his assistant. In 1943, with Keaton serving stateside as a flight instructor in the Army Air Corps, Swayze soloed on the Sunday *Flyin' Jenny.* Swayze filled in on both the daily and Sunday strips when Keaton became ill and died tragically young in 1945. The presence of paper dolls in a comic strip usually indicates a large female readership.

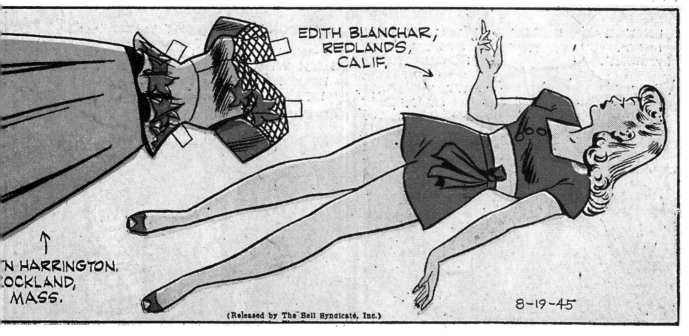

66. Left: Fawcett editor Rod Reed assigned artist Marc Swayze to create the design for Mary Marvel. Reed was also a versatile writer. He wrote some of the funniest Mary Marvel and Captain Marvel stories, as well as action and adventure scripts for other Fawcett heroes like Spy Smasher and Nyoka, the Jungle Girl. The Fawcett crew worked hard and played hard, gathering on weekends and after hours for baseball or bowling and partying. This photo was taken at a gathering in Reed's house in Malverne, Long Island; Reed is at left, Swayze is playing guitar, and Reed's wife, Kentucky, is at right. (*Circa.* 1942.)

67. Otto Binder observed that the keynote of the Marvel family stories was "humor, fantasy, and whimsy," with Captain Marvel himself enjoying the nickname, "The Big Cheese." Many Marvel stories were parodies of literary works, myths, and even other comics. In Mary Marvel's stories, fantasy often received the strongest emphasis, as in this delightful example where Mary assists a group of Gnomes. (*Wow Comics* no. 33, February 1945.)

68. More fantasy from Mary Marvel's *Wow Comics* adventures. The male gnomes have been kidnapped by a circus, and their women have been stealing jewelry in order to rescue them. (*Wow Comics* no. 40, January 1946.)

69. "Mary Marvel Copies a Cowboy." In addition to joining Mary Marvel's club, girls could dress like their heroine by ordering fashions she endorsed through the mail. (*Wow Comics* no. 56, July 1947.)

70. The Fawcett editors obviously knew that Mary Marvel's readers included large numbers of girls. Although all the backup features in *Wow Comics* featured male heroes, advertisements for the Mary Marvel Club ran for a number of years in *Wow*, inviting girls to send in their dimes to become members. (*Wow Comics* no. 56, July 1947.)

71. Mary Marvel advertises *Mechanix Illustrated*. The other members of the Marvel Family depicted here include Captain Marvel (top), Captain Marvel, Junior (lower left), and Hoppy, the Marvel Bunny (lower right). (*Wow Comics* no. 40, January 1946.)

In addition to appearing in her brother's book, Mary could be found from 1945 to 1954 in *Marvel Family Comics,* along with Captain Marvel and their adopted brother, Captain Marvel Junior, a crippled newsboy who said Captain Marvel's name in order to attain his own superpowers. The Shazam girl also starred in *Wow Comics,* beginning with issue no. 10, and had her own comic book, *Mary Marvel Comics,* from 1945 to 1948. By the time Mary's publisher, Fawcett Comics, ceased publication in 1954, Mary Marvel had appeared in 172 comic books, more comics than any other superheroine except Wonder Woman. She was truly the world's mightiest girl.

They have rightly named you . . . *Lady Satan* . . . *Aaaggghh!*

—Nazi agent to Lady Satan, *Dynamic Comics* no. 3 (1942)

CHAPTER
5

The strong fantasy, myth, and fairy tale themes in *Wonder Woman* were a major reason for the character's popularity with young girls. The same can be said of Mary Marvel. Girls and women have a strong preference for fantasy. In the field of science fiction writing, where a great many women are represented, it is the women who, by and large, write the fantasy books (and it is the women who read them!), while the majority of "hard science" is written by men.

Elements of myth, fantasy, and the supernatural abounded in superheroine comics of the forties and fifties. Often the supernatural

I'M NOT ON EARTH NOW, BUT AS SOON AS I LEARN OF EVIL WHICH MUST BE MET WITH QUICK PUNISHMENT, I SHALL TRAVEL THE GREAT DISTANCE AND RETURN TO YOUR PEOPLE TO TREAT THEM TO -- *DEATH*!

72. The supernatural heroine The Black Widow was Claire Voyant, a beautiful blonde murder victim sent back to earth by Satan himself. Dressed in black tights, boots, and a scarlet cape, she dispatched the souls of evildoers to hell in adventures written by George Kapitan and drawn by, among others, Stan Drake, who was later the artist of the romantic syndicated newspaper strip, *The Heart of Juliet Jones.* (*Mystic Comics* no. 7, 1941.)

heroines were darker characters than their more patriotic sisters. The Black Widow, for instance, emerged from hell itself to appear in three different comic books—*USA, All-Select,* and the aptly named *Mystic,* from 1940 until 1943. The Black Widow was drawn by Stan Drake, who later became successful with a much more cheerful newspaper strip, *The Heart of Juliet Jones.* Dressed in black tights and a scarlet cape, the Black Widow, a beautiful blonde with a hypnotic stare, is a kind of avenging dark angel. Satan himself sends for her, because there are some people on Earth who are "so evil that I will not wait for their souls!" Since she is not human, neither bullets nor acid thrown at her can stop her. Once she has covered the intended victim with her cape, he

lies dead at her feet and, "her work done, the Black Widow fades away and makes the long journey back to Satan—"

The early superheroines usually brought their foes to justice with a minimum of blood, or if the villains died, it was often because of a propitious accident. But darker heroines like the Black Widow actually killed. Although her name would suggest a supernatural origin, "the mysterious Lady Satan" was a human superheroine who was otherwise similar to the Black Widow. Her adventures in *Dynamic Comics* and *Red Seal Comics* lasted from 1941 until 1947. In a 1942 story, the masked woman in the slinky dress kills a Nazi who has disguised himself as Charles de Gaulle in order to assassinate Franklin Roosevelt and Winston Churchill. Roosevelt and Churchill wish to thank her—Churchill says, "A clever woman . . . and a brave one"—but as is usual for superheroines, she has no time to be thanked by great heads of state. "There is important work for me in Paris," she says. "I cannot delay any longer." Churchill and Roosevelt wave to her departing plane, and Roosevelt comments, "Perhaps some day her fight for liberty and justice will not have been in vain."

Like the Black Widow, Ghost Woman was not human. She was killed in an auto accident at the start of her origin story and spent the rest of the story in spectral form, battling malevolent supernatural forces. Unfortunately, Ghost Woman made only one appearance in *Star Studded Comics,* in 1944, but in 1993 Dark Horse Comics published a version for the 1990s, simply called *Ghost.*

Wildfire, whose adventures started in *Smash Comics* in 1941 and lasted a year, also was not quite human. She appeared to be a kind of elemental fire creature. Artist Jim Mooney, just out of art school, patterned her after his first wife, who had long red hair, but he added little flames which rose from her forehead in place of bangs. A story in *Smash* no. 36 shows Wildfire giving a container of fire, which resembles a glorified cigarette lighter, to a little boy. She tells him that he can use it when he needs to call her. Surprisingly, Jim Mooney does not recall receiving any letters from irate parents, complaining that his superheroine encouraged their children to set their hair on fire or to play with cigarette lighters!

Unlike Ghost Woman, Phantom Lady was supernatural in name only. This costumed heroine

73. Lady Satan, a masked figure in a slinky black dress, was a dark superheroine of the 1940s whose adventures were created by artists including George Tuska. She appeared in *Dynamic* and *Red Seal Comics.* (*Dynamic Comics* no. 3, 1942.)

74. Ghost Woman appeared in only one story in *Star Studded* comics; killed in an auto accident, she fights supernatural forces that menace the living. In this sequence, she realizes that she is dead. (*Star Studded*, 1944.)

originated in the first issue of *Police Comics* in 1941. Like Marla Drake in *Miss Fury*, Phantom Lady is a rich girl when she isn't fighting crime. The first panel of Phantom Lady's first story reads: "The society columns record the activities of Sandra Knight, debutante daughter of Senator Henry Knight . . . no one suspects that the frivolous Sandra is also *The Phantom Lady,* whose battle against spies and public enemies constantly make headlines . . ."

Artist Arthur Peddy designed her in a yellow costume with green cape, and gave her a kind of reverse flashlight, her black ray, which blinded people. She also came with the requisite boyfriend, State Department investigator Don Borden, who, even though Sandra Knight and Phantom Lady looked exactly alike—she didn't even wear a mask!—never caught on. Superheroine comics have definitely supplied us with the dumbest private detectives, cops, and investigators in the universe.

In 1946, Phantom Lady got a new publisher, Fox Comics, and her own book. She also got a complete new look, with a blue costume and red cape. Her new artist, Matt Baker, one of the rare African American artists in comics during the forties, excelled in drawing women. It has been argued by male writers that Baker's women were drawn to appeal to men, and while that is certainly probable, they also appealed strongly to a female audience. His dashing and glamorous women have a kind of forties movie star appeal. He also had a flair for fashion, and paid loving attention to details of clothing and hair styles. During Baker's all-too-brief life—he died prematurely from a congenital heart condition—he drew jungle queens, aviatrixes, girl detectives, and superheroines; they were always beautiful and always strong.

Phantom Lady was at her most interesting when she interacted with other women, and this happened often in her stories. In "The Condemned Venus," from *Phantom Lady* no. 14, 1947, she actually gets herself arrested and put into prison so that she can free her friend Kitty Manders, who has been condemned to death for murder. Together, on the lam from the law like Thelma and Louise, they find the real killers.

75. Wildfire appeared in *Smash Comics* nos. 25–37, and was the creation of versatile artist Jim Mooney, who drew superheroes for Marvel and DC into the 1970s, and pulp novelist Robert Turner, who later became a writer of crime and mystery TV scripts. Red-haired Carol Vance Martin, secret identity of this Human Torch–like hero, was patterned by Mooney after his first wife. (*Smash Comics* no. 36, 1941.)

76. In her first incarnation, Phantom Lady was just one of the secondary heroes in Quality's *Police Comics,* in which the headliners included Jack Cole's Plastic Man and Will Eisner's Spirit. Artist Arthur Peddy designed her yellow costume with a green cape, and she was equipped with a black ray that shed a blinding darkness on pursuers. (*Police Comics,* 1941.)

"A Shroud for the Bride," in the same issue, is a kind of dark Cinderella story. Porky Mead, an alcoholic millionaire, attends a masquerade ball with a pretty waitress he has picked up. A shot rings out and his date falls to the ground, dead. Phantom Lady learns that the victim was wearing a costume meant for someone else—one of three jealous women who had been stood up by Porky. Stealing the dead girl's shoe, she tries it on each of the women, knowing the shoe will fit the murderer.

Thanks to Matt Baker's gorgeous art, *Phantom Lady* lasted until 1949. That year, another debutante turned superheroine had her own comic book. In 1940, society girl Brenda Banks covered the bottom half of her face with a filmy green scarf and became the crime-fighting Lady Luck. Aside from her name, there was nothing particularly mystic about this heroine, whose light and humorous adventures were drawn by Chuck Mazoujian, Gill Fox, and Klaus Nordling. Lady Luck started as a backup feature to Will Eisner's masked hero, the Spirit, in special Sunday newspaper comic sections, but in 1949 and 1950 she graduated to her own book.

Lady Luck is not to be confused with Lady Fairplay, who appeared in *Bang-Up Comics*

77. Other artists drew Phantom Lady during her time at Quality, including Frank Borth, who lowered the neckline of her costume, and Rudy Palais. But her most famous incarnation was created by African American artist Matt Baker, who combined a masterful pinup style with inventive page designs and striking cinematic perspective to create memorable stories for Fox Features Syndicate when it revived the character in her own book in August 1947; she also appeared in Fox's *All Top Comics*. (*Phantom Lady,* 1947.)

78. *Phantom Lady* has been controversial since Fredric Wertham reproduced one of its covers in *Seduction of the Innocent* (1954), and Baker's lovely women, regularly depicted in lingerie, were certainly part of its appeal. But Baker's talent encompassed superb, fast-paced storytelling, and the best stories were those in which Phantom Lady's costars were other women, as in this excerpt from "Condemned Venus" in which Sandra Knight rescues her friend, Kitty Manders. (*Phantom Lady* no. 14, 1947.)

79. Matt Baker had a flair for fashion illustration that included detailed and convincing depictions of hair styles and clothing. (Unlike other heroines, Phantom Lady performed her athletic feats in flats, not heels.) In this page, also from "Condemned Venus," Phantom Lady gets herself arrested so that she can free Kitty Manders. (*Phantom Lady* no. 14, 1947.)

80. A splash page by Matt Baker showing Phantom Lady using her black ray, from the Cinderella-inspired story, "A Shroud for the Bride." (*Phantom Lady* no. 14, 1947; reprinted in *Daring Adventures* no. 12, 1963.)

81. In 1940, Will Eisner made comic history when he created the first and only weekly comic book distributed through newspapers. The comic book was named after its lead feature, *The Spirit,* but it included two other continuing features, *Lady Luck* and *Mr. Mystic.* Another debutante turned crime fighter, Lady Luck dressed all in green. She was drawn by Chuck Mazoujian and Nick Viscardi in the first and second years of the strip, but her best-known adventures are those drawn by Klaus Nordling in the *Spirit* newspaper sections and *Smash Comics;* with issue no. 86, *Smash* became *Lady Luck* for the last year of its run, 1949–1950. (Art by Klaus Nordling, 1946.)

THE INCREDIBLE FEATS OF LADY FAIRPLAY DURING THE PAST FEW WEEKS HAVE SENT THE UNDERWORLD RUNNING FOR COVER. CRIME HAS BEEN REDUCED TO A MINIMUM IN THIS CITY. GANGSTERS LIVE IN MORTAL TERROR OF THIS FEMALE DYNAMO. LITTLE DO THEY REALIZE THAT THIS REMARKABLE LADY IS REALLY A MODEST YOUNG SCHOOL TEACHER WHOSE TRUE NAME IS MARY LEE . . . .

TODAY, WE FIND MARY DRIVING THROUGH THE COUNTRY-SIDE AFTER A TRYING DAY IN HER CLASS ROOM.

IT'S A RELIEF TO GET OUT IN THE OPEN SPACES FOR A CHANGE. THIS FRESH AIR MAKES A PERSON FEEL LIKE A MILLION!

OH! OH! I SPOKE TOO SOON! IT'S BEGINNING TO RAIN —

82. Lady Fairplay appeared in only three issues of *Bang-Up Comics;* she was a crime fighter created by Jack Ryan, who had been an assistant to Chester Gould on *Dick Tracy.* (*Bang-Up Comics* no. 2, 1942.)

83. Magga the Magnificent says the magic words. (*Atoman Comics* no. 2, 1946.)

Amazing-Man Comics in 1941 and 1942. Lucille Martin, "an adventurous novelist," is on a ship returning from China when she is accosted by a beautiful Chinese woman named Lotus, who gives her a ring with a mystic blue stone, explaining that "it possesses superhuman powers." That night, Lotus is killed by unknown assassins, leaving Lucille to discover that the blue stone contains a magical gas which gives her super strength. She fashions a blue costume and mask, declaring, "Henceforth I will be known as 'the Blue Lady,'" and proceeds to have adventures involving Chinatown, opium, and a mysterious jade statuette.

It's a magic moonstone that gives Moon Girl "the strength of ten ordinary men and guards her against all harm." This memorable heroine starred in her own book for two years, and was drawn by Sheldon Moldoff, who also had drawn

84. Forty-five years before Kathleen Turner's character in *Romancing the Stone*, adventurous novelist Lucille Martin encountered a mysterious blue stone set in a ring that gave her super strength. The color of the stone inspired her to make a blue costume and to select the name Blue Lady; her feature appeared in *Amazing-Man Comics* nos. 24–26. (*Amazing-Man Comics*, 1941.)

during its three-issue run, in 1941 and 1942. Her story tells us that "gangsters live in terror of this female dynamo. Little do they realize that this remarkable lady is really a modest young school teacher whose true name is Mary Lee . . ." Mary takes down her prim hair style and removes her glasses before donning an almost fairy-tale princess type of costume, complete with tiara and chain-mail skirt. Jack Ryan, Lady Fairplay's artist, was an assistant to Dick Tracy's creator, Chester Gould, and the superheroine's strip displays the same clean, simple style that could be seen in Dick Tracy. The strip also features some of the best examples of comic book–style sound effects ever seen before the advent of pop art, my particular favorite being "Socko!"

Sometimes the heroine received her powers from a mystic source, like Magga the Magnificent, who got hers from Tibet. In her 1946 appearance in *Atoman Comics*, radio star Kay, whose last name is never given, calls, "Om mani padme hum!" "And the echo of these strange words," reads the caption, "in a far off Tibetan Lamasary transforms Kay . . . into Magga . . . maiden of miraculous might!" The comic goes on to tell us that "Magga can fly with the speed of thought!"

And sometimes it is a mystic jewel that is responsible for the transformation. A ring plays that part in The Blue Lady, which ran in

MOON GIRL AND THE PRINCE

85. Moon Girl was actually from Tamerlane's legendary capital, Samarkand, and not from the moon. She was created by Max Gaines and modeled on his earlier success, Wonder Woman. Her origin story was penned by prolific comic scripter and science fiction novelist Gardner F. Fox (b. 1911). (*Moon Girl* no. 1, 1947.)

the more forgettable sidekick, Hawkgirl. Maggie Thompson, editor of the comics industry weekly tabloid, *The Comics Buyer's Guide,* recalls her fascination as a five year old with the exotic heroine: "For months [after reading the comic] the women I drew had the same chokers with the precious stones and the lace-up sandals with turned-up toes [as Moon Girl]. I must have considered this the ideal accouterment to decorate whatever females I drew."

Moon Girl was published by Max Gaines, who had been the first publisher of *Wonder Woman.* By 1947, apparently regretting that he had let the amazing Amazon go to National Comics (later called DC Comics), he felt the need to once more produce a myth-inspired superheroine. "The princess of the moon," as she was called, was not from the moon at all but from Samarkand, and even without her magic moonstone, she was a superior creature. According to her very

MOON GIRL AND THE PRINCE

86. A magic moonstone, worn on a choker, gives Moon Girl her power. In the first issue, she bests dashing Prince Mengu in a series of contests–and wins his heart. Together they dedicate themselves to fighting evil and she adopts the secret identity of Clare Lune, but unfortunately the book soon lost its fantasy focus, first becoming a crime, then a romance book before being canceled with issue no. 12. (*Moon Girl* no. 1, 1947.)

romantic origin story by Gardner Fox, the saga of Moon Girl started just before World War II. The princess lived in what appeared to be a matriarchy; at any rate, there were no men in evidence. She is taming a wild horse when we first see her, and one of her ladies-in-waiting comments, "No living thing is a match for the moon girl!" "Among her admirers," we are told, "is the handsome Prince Mengu . . ." The prince, whom artist Moldoff based on film star Victor Mature, thinks, "What a woman! I came a thousand miles to find her, and she shall be my wife!"

end of Atalanta. But Moon Girl, with the magic moonstone around her neck, proved to be invincible, and the prince lost the contest. As she watches him ride off on his horse, the princess has second thoughts: "He's leaving the castle . . . forever!" She goes to her mother: "I've driven him away and I—I love him!"

The queen tells her to go after the prince: "Find your loved one! Perhaps you can still win him back!" But the next caption reads, "But he is not to be found in Samarkand, nor in his own kingdom of Mengu."

87. Sheldon Moldoff began his career in comics assisting Bob Kane on *Batman*, then leapt to prominence at nineteen as the artist of Hawkman in *Flash Comics*. He rapidly absorbed the style and grace of Alex Raymond's artwork for the *Flash Gordon* and *Jungle Jim* comic strips, leading him to create striking and atmospheric Hawkman stories, followed by similarly powerful work on *Moon Girl*. (*Moon Girl* no. 2, Winter 1947.)

It was never specified, but the prince probably was Greek. Later in the story, he tells Moon Girl, "I am of the blood of Hercules!"

Moon Girl was not as eager for marriage as the prince. She tells her mother, the queen, "I do not know this man! I cannot love him . . . and he shall not be my husband!" The queen tells her: "It is decreed that the man who takes you for his wife must first prove his superior strength!" and she gives her daughter the moonstone. "Once you wear the moonstone, no man will be your master!" she declares.

The contest between Moon Girl and the prince which followed borrows a little from Wonder Woman and a little from the Greek leg-

Princesses, of course, do not give up that easily, and Prince Mengu is finally discovered in America, where he has "found a position as athletic coach in a college . . ." He doesn't recognize the princess in her American disguise, when she finds him on the campus and challenges him to a shotputting match. "A girl!" he exclaims. "What would you know about shotputting?" But of course she beats him, and he realizes who she must be: "Only one person in the world could equal that throw! Why, you must be. . . ."

By now the prince is unwilling to leave his new country. He wants to stay in America, "using my strength only to fight evil . . ." This is okay with Moon Girl, who takes the pseudonym Clare

88. Mysta of the Moon was one of the strong women heroes that were often featured in comics published by Fiction House, and the only one who was a true superheroine. Fiction House employed more women artists than any other comics company in the 1940s, and here the goddesslike heroine is rendered by Fran Hopper. (*Planet Comics* no. 38, September 1945.)

89. Mysta of the Moon was transferred from her home planet to Earth, where she assumed a secret identity as Ana Thane, a technician working for the Safety Council. Among the artists who drew Mysta were Maurice Whitman and Matt Baker, who, in these later stories, drew her as a slender, silver-haired woman. (*Planet Comics* no. 56, September 1948.)

Lune and stays with him, dedicating herself to "the task of creating a better world!"

It is easy to see why Moon Girl's costume fascinated little Maggie Thompson. Sheldon Moldoff designed an outfit for the princess that, while inspired by Asian clothing, also echoed the moon itself. Her collar, the toes of her strappy sandals, and even the cuffs of her shorts all curve upwards like the quarter-moon design that decorates the shorts. Moldoff based the princess's exotic looks on actress Merle Oberon, but exaggerated her widow's peak and gave her short, upward-curving eyebrows. The effect is otherworldly. Moon Girl looked as if she might very well have come from the moon, and many of her stories had a planetary theme. She uttered exclamations like "Great Pluto!" and "Saturn, fill my legs with power!" and battled women from the planet Venus.

If Moon Girl's creators had stuck with their dashing beginnings, they probably would have had a long-lasting hit, but they appear to have been unable to leave well enough alone. During the two-year run of the book, her writers and editors, trying to keep up with each new fad in comics, vacillated between putting out a fantasy comic book and putting out a crime comic. Even in the first issue, along with the tale of Moon Girl's mythic origins and a story about Venusian women, there was a very run-of-the-mill story in which the exotic heroine fights smugglers. Any hero or heroine could fight smugglers, but only Moon Girl had archenemies like "Erica with her wolf-girls from Venus"! By issue no. 7, the book's title had changed to *Moon Girl Fights Crime,* and by no. 9, in response to the burgeoning love comic genre, it had metamorphosed into a romance comic called *A Moon, A Girl . . . Romance.* Too bad.

Mysta of the Moon really was from the moon. A mysterious goddesslike figure who advised and controlled the universe from her headquarters on the moon, she appeared regularly in *Planet Comics. Planet* was one of six titles published by Fiction House, one of the most remarkable comic book publishers of the forties and fifties. Not only did this company employ more women than any other comic publisher—artists like Fran Hopper, Lily Renee, Marcia Snyder, and Ruth Atkinson—

but most of their pulp-style action stories either starred or featured strong, beautiful, competent heroines. They were war nurses, aviatrixes, girl detectives, counterspies, and animal skin–clad jungle queens, and they were in command. Guns blazing, daggers unsheathed, sword in hand, they leaped across the pages, ready to take on any villain. And they did not need rescuing.

However, only Mysta, out of all these wonderful women, qualifies as a superheroine. She is, the story tells us, "sole possessor of the scientific knowledge of the universe." In her 1945 origin story, she was given that knowledge by a scientist, Dr. Kort, in his moon laboratory. The good doctor then conveniently died, leaving Mysta alone on the moon. There, accompanied only by her faithful robot who obeys her telepathic commands, she attempts to bring peace and culture to the universe. At first Mysta was drawn by Fran Hopper as a blonde, but later artists gave her silver hair, as befitted her association with our silvery satellite.

By 1948, Mysta had left the moon for the Earth and a more traditional superhero situation. At this point she was depicted, by Matt Baker, with her long silver hair tied back in little side ponytails—perhaps as a disguise? Posing as "technician grade three" Ana Thane, Mysta now worked for the Safety Council under the direction of handsome but clueless Dirk Garro. When a mysterious box arrived at the Safety Council, he was advised, "You'd best clear it with Mysta!" The bullheaded Garro answered, "*Mysta?* A Woman? Is she head of this Safety Council or am I? I'll have no need of her—*ever!*" Of course, giant insects emerged from the box and started eating up everybody on Earth. Only Mysta, in her technician guise, could save the planet.

These stories usually ended with Mysta saving the day and Garro taking the credit. In the last panel, he looks at her thoughtfully and speculates, "That technician—hmmm . . . I wonder . . ." But of course, as in all superheroine stories, he never was able to come to the obvious conclusion. Meanwhile, Mysta, flashing a Mona Lisa smile at the reader, thinks, "Oh well, it doesn't matter, so long as Dirk Garro never discovers he owes his life to Mysta!"

That dome is atom-bomb proof and keeps the temperature at an even 72.6 degrees at all times.

–Atoma, *Joe Palooka* comics no. 15 (1947)

CHAPTER
6

Although many wartime superheroines did not survive the war, the costumed heroine was hardly defunct. New and different postwar super-women emerged in the second half of the forties, reflecting the dawn of the nuclear age. Atoma, who appeared only once in the back pages of *Joe Palooka* comics, typified the 1947 belief in a utopian atomic future. Artist Bob Powell designed her futuristic outfit complete with goggles and such items as "electronic directional flight control (EDF)," "nylon-xenton wings (for added flight control)," and a short-skirted dress made of "celanese-phreton cloth." The flying heroine is an historian from the year 2446 who lives in the dome-covered "City of Peace" where "energo-armo robots" are controlled by radar, people live to be at least 250 years old, and a "spectro-ray chamber" kills any germs one may have picked up outside the dome. But things are not all well in the domed city: there is no freedom, and citizens need special passes to move about freely. Alas, we will never know how Atoma fought for freedom in her dystopia. On the first page of her story was an editor's note that asked: "Do you think we should run 'Atoma' as a regular feature or would you prefer 'Flyin' Fool'?" Sadly, the readers evidently preferred Flyin' Fool, because Atoma was never seen again.

Ultra Violet was another new type of super-heroine, appearing in what was then a new type of comic book. Romance comics were just getting started in 1947, and *My Date*, a very early romance comic produced by the team of Joe Simon and Jack Kirby, was not yet typical of that genre. Along with "true" love stories like "Date Snatcher," the comic book included humorous comics about teen characters like the infamous House-date Harry who, instead of taking girls out on dates, hangs around their houses and empties their refrigerators. Also included were the adventures of Violet Ray, a postwar bobby-soxer whose "dreams are indistinguishable from reality" and who has the ability to daydream herself into a sophisticated older woman named Ultra Violet. The stories were drawn by Dan Barry, who later drew the long-running newspaper strip *Flash Gordon*. Nobody wears any costumes in these lighthearted adventures, but Violet's unusual powers qualify her as a superheroine.

A more traditional postwar superheroine was Miss Masque. Like Phantom Lady, Miss Fury,

and Lady Luck, all of whom survived the war, Miss Masque was a society debutante in real life. Each story featured an introductory text reminiscent of those in *Phantom Lady:* "Nobody in society's four hundred knows that their most popular debutante and darling of the society columnists, Diane Adams, is also the glamorous lady of mystery—the scourge of the underworld—none other than the one and only Miss Masque!" Comics in the forties seemed to be full of superheroes and -heroines masquerading as society people, perhaps because it's easier for those without a day job to sleep late after battling bad guys all night.

Miss Masque first appeared in *Exciting Comics* in 1946, but a year later she had moved to

90. Violet Ray and her friend Lucy Benson are two typical teenage, postwar bobbysoxers, whose major concerns are boys, dates, and high school. Violet, however, in her secret identity as Ultra Violet, can become any sort of adult woman she desires through the power of her daydreams. (*My Date Comics* no. 3, November 1947.)

America's Best Comics, where she stayed until 1949. Along with her move came a costume change. Artist Lin Streeter had originally clothed his blonde heroine in a cape, gloves, and short red dress with the initials MM sideways on her chest. He topped this outfit off with a fedora that bore one M on its brim. By 1947, although she kept the cape and gloves, she had switched to a stylish, midriff-baring shorts outfit and a skullcap.

Debutante Diane put on—surprise!—a mask to become Miss Masque. Her stories excelled in snappy dialogue. The superheroine says, "I may wear skirts—but brother, I've got plenty of

ELECTRONIC
DIRECTIONAL
FLIGHT
CONTROL
(EDF)

POLARIZED
GLASSES

EARPHONES

ATOMIC FUEL
CONTAINER

CELANESE-
PHRETON
CLOTH

ATOMIC JET
PROPULSION
TUBES
(AP TUBES)

NYLON-XENTON
WINGS (FOR)
ADDED FLIGHT
CONTROL)

TWO-WAY
TELEPHONIC
RADIO

AUXILIARY ATOM
FUEL TANK

91. Atoma, probably the only superheroine who was an historian by
profession, flew in a backup feature in one issue of Harvey Comics'
Joe Palooka. This story depicted
the world of A.D. 2446 as technolog-
ically advanced but socially repres-
sive, and was drawn by Bob Powell
(*circa* 1917–1967), who also had
drawn such powerful women as
Harvey's Black Cat, jungle queen
Sheena, and Lady Luck (as well as
the Spirit himself) for Will Eisner.
(*Joe Palooka* comics no. 15, 1947.)

92. Ultra Violet was probably the most unique heroine to appear in the romance comics of the 1940s, because the teenage protagonist used her daydreams to experience a variety of adult women's roles. Artist Dan Barry (b. 1923) would later draw the daily and Sunday *Flash Gordon* strips. (*My Date Comics* no. 3, November 1947.)

punch!," and as she uses that "plenty of punch" on a crook's jaw, he exclaims, "You're no lady— you're *dynamite! Ooooof!*"

Miss Masque's adventures, like those of many other postwar heroines, included humor that had been lacking in earlier adventure comics. Perhaps Nazis had been nothing to chuckle about, but the new comics reflected plucky postwar optimism.

Another blonde masked heroine who was born in 1946—Blonde Phantom—was the first of four blonde superheroines, all created for the same publisher within a space of two years, all starring in their own books, all possessing elements of myth or fantasy, and all aimed directly at young female readers. The publisher was the Marvel Comics Group under editor Stan Lee.

93. Ultra Violet's transformations were often dramatic, and would have resonated with teenage girls whose bodies were growing and changing. (*My Date Comics* no. 3, November 1947.)

AS ALWAYS, VI'S DREAMS ARE INDISTINGUISHABLE FROM REALITY, AND SHE STARTS TO BECOME HER DREAM-SELF...THIS TIME A SOPHISTICATED-EXECUTIVE TYPE...

I'D PERSONALLY SUPERVISE THE BABY-SITTING DIVISION... WISE, MOTHERLY...

BELLBOTTOMS WOULD BEG.. BUT LITERALLY *PLEAD* WITH ME.. JUST ONE DANCE.. BUT I'D REFUSE FOR THE CHILDREN'S SAKE!

94. In the Ultra Violet stories, Violet's transformations were often rendered with dramatic effects. (*My Date Comics* no. 3, November 1947.)

Marvel Comics had already been successfully publishing comic books for girls since they put out the *Miss America* comic book and magazine in 1944. That same year saw the debut of another girl-oriented comic character, Tessie the Typist. Patsy Walker, who had started in the pages of *Miss America Magazine,* got her own book in 1945, as did Millie the Model and Nellie the Nurse. Having covered all possible careers for girls (except perhaps Betty the Brain Surgeon), Stan Lee decided to try something more serious in 1946, and he came up with Blonde Phantom, drawn by Syd Shores and written by the ever-prolific Otto Binder.

Except for the fact that she fought crime while wearing an improbable outfit consisting of a slinky red evening gown and matching open-toed pumps, Blonde Phantom was the most traditional of her four supersisters. In her civilian disguise as Louise Grant, private secretary to detective Mark Mason, she, like so many other superheroines, pinned her hair back in a prim chignon and affected harlequin glasses. As Blonde Phantom, she pulled out the bobby pins and traded the glasses for a mask. And, like so

many superheroines' love interests, Mark Mason was a pretty poor detective, because he never made the connection between the superheroine he adored and the secretary who secretly adored him. This Superman–Lois Lane–Clark Kent type triangle actually led Louise Grant to be jealous of herself. In a short comic story called "I Hate Me," Louise, dateless as usual, falls asleep while reading a romance magazine and dreams that she is in Mark Mason's arms. Just as he is declaring his love ("Oh, Louise, I love you! I've *always* loved you!"), Blonde Phantom enters the picture. He immediately deserts Louise for the superheroine (who is, of course, also Louise), murmuring to her, "I love you, beautiful! I've *always* loved you!" Louise wakes up and, holding her Blonde Phantom costume at arm's length, addresses it: "Oh, why don't you stay out of my dreams?"

Two years after her debut, Blonde Phantom was joined by Namora, Sun Girl, and Venus. Namora had originated in comics as just another sidekick; she was first introduced as the cousin of Prince Namor, the Submariner. But in 1948, she starred in three issues of her own book. Artist Bill Everett, who had created Submariner, dressed her in a bathing suit made of fish scales and put wings on her ankles, although the wings seemed to come and go throughout the strip. The logic in Namora's stories is a mite shaky, but Bill Everett's art is great. Namora, described in the stories' subtitle as "The Sea Beauty," seems to be able to appear wherever there is water. Thus, in her first issue, she emerges from a river in the Yucatan to star in a kind of jungle girl adventure, while later in the book she shows up in the China Seas and fights diamond smugglers.

Sun Girl received the apt appelation, "The Mysterious Beauty." The mystery was her origin and her special powers, neither of which were ever explained during her comic book's three-issue run. Although she didn't appear to have actually come from the sun, she did wear a bright yellow costume and was given to using expressions such as, "Whirling sun balls!", "Great

95. Miss Masque appeared in Best Comics' *America's Best Comics, Exciting Comics, Fighting Yank,* and *Black Terror* titles; she was debutante Diane Adams who donned a mask to become a wisecracking whirlwind of a crime fighter in stories that mixed action with humor. She is shown here as drawn by Lin Streeter, who also drew Pat Patriot. She also was drawn by Bob Oksner (b. 1916), an artist equally adept at superhero and humor comics. (*Exciting Comics*, 1946 and 1947.)

96. Between 1946 and 1948, four new blonde superheroines were created for Marvel Comics titles: Blonde Phantom, Namora, Sun Girl, and Venus. The first was Blonde Phantom, created by Stan Lee with her initial stories scripted by the prolific Otto Binder. She had her own book, which ran for ten issues between 1946 and 1949, and her stories also appeared in seven other Marvel titles. (1948.)

solar aspect was enough to connect the two superbeings.

The strangest and longest-lasting of these four superheroines was Venus, who survived for twenty issues. Venus actually was from the planet Venus, and she was also the ancient Roman goddess of the same name. Twenty-odd years before Marvel comics introduced Thor and Hercules to the comics pages, Venus was the very first deity to star in her own book as a superpowered character.

Venus's first story introduces us to the goddess, ruler of a futuristic Venusian city. Dressed in high-heeled sandals and a white toga with floating blue panels, she wanders through the halls of her "castle of the Gods on Mt. Lustre," and complains, "How many centuries have I ruled this planet! How weary I am of the life I lead! How I would trade this lonely, barren existence for just a normal life on the planet Earth!" And wishing appears to make it so. "In a split second, millions of miles between the two planets melted into nothingness and time stood still as the heavens trembled!" runs the poetic caption over a panel in which Venus floats Earthward through the starry cosmos.

The goddess lands on Earth in the middle of a busy city street, causing a traffic jam. There she is spotted by Whitney

sunfires!", and "Trembling sun spots!" Sun Girl's chief gimmick seems to have been her "sunbeam," a kind of superflashlight that she wore on her wrist, although in issue no. 1, she briefly carried an emergency pouch from which she extracted a lariat and a "portable electric tracer." Sun Girl also appears to have been the first superheroine without a secret identity, not counting women like Namora or the Black Widow, who are not really human. Although Sun Girl only lasted through 1948, she was paired with the Human Torch in 1949, in his own book and in *Marvel Mystery Comics*. Although Sun Girl never "flamed on," perhaps her

THIS STRIP WAS DRAWN BY SYD SHORES THE TALENTED ARTIST WHO BRINGS YOU THE "BLONDE PHANTOM" AND "CAPTAIN AMERICA" EVERY MONTH!

97. Sydney Lawrence "Syd" Shores (1918–1973), artist on Blonde Phantom, drew stories for Marvel Comics from the 1940s to the year of his death. (Caricature by Ken Bald, 1947.)

98. Like many superheroines, Blonde Phantom held a secretarial position, working as gal Friday Louise Grant to private detective Mark Mason. The eternal triangle of boss, secretary, and glamorous woman of mystery led Louise to be jealous of herself in the memorable Blonde Phantom story, "I Hate Me." (*Blonde Phantom,* 1948.)

Hammond, publisher of *Beauty Magazine,* who has been thinking, "There must be a new idea somewhere which I can use in *Beauty Magazine . . .* something different, fresh, exciting!" Although Hammond doesn't really believe the beautiful blonde when she insists that she is the goddess Venus, he knows a good gimmick when he sees one, and by the end of the story he has made her editor of *Beauty Magazine.* ("With your looks, the

magazine will be a huge success if we just run pictures of you and nothing else!")

Stan Lee, who wrote the first batch of Venus stories, merrily mixed his mythology. In issue no. 4, in a story titled "Whom the Gods Would Destroy" (not the last time Stan Lee was to use that title!), Venus brings the biblical hero Sampson back to Earth with her. He is represented as being one of the gods from Mount

99. The first popular golden-age superheroes to follow Superman were the Human Torch and Namor, the Sub-Mariner; their origin stories appeared in *Marvel Comics* no. 1 (October–November 1939). Bill Everett (1917–1973) created Namor and, nine years later, Namora, the Sea Beauty, who was Namor's long-lost cousin. Her origin story in *Marvel Mystery* no. 82 (May 1947) was not by Everett, but he designed the character and her costume and wrote and drew the stories in her own short-lived comic book, which lasted only three issues. (*Namora* no. 1, August 1948.)

100. The Human Torch had a kid sidekick named Toro, but he was dropped in favor of Sun Girl, the Mysterious Beauty, when she joined the flaming superhero in *Marvel Mystery Comics* no. 88. Sun Girl's sunbeam was the inverse of Phantom Lady's black ray, a kind of powerful flashlight worn on her wrist that blinded and confused the bad guys. (*Marvel Mystery* no. 89, 1948.)

Olympus, along with Apollo, Mars, and Bacchus. In no. 5, she has a run-in with the Norse god Loki, and in issue no. 10, she is threatened by the son of the Judeo-Christian Satan.

Venus's stories also changed in genre through the years. The first few issues followed Stan Lee's lighter formula for his teenage girl comics: a love triangle between two girls and a guy. Whitney Hammond's secretary, Della, covets the job of editor, and also covets Hammond himself. When Venus gets the job she wanted, and seems likely also to get Hammond, Della attempts to sabotage her rival. These early stories were drawn by Ed Winiarsky, who also drew Hedy Devine, one of the teen comics. Indeed, Venus, as drawn by Ed Winiarsky, looked almost exactly like Hedy Devine. But soon the comic took a more romantic tone, featuring stories like "The Romance That Could Not Be" and "The Man she Dared Not Love." These were drawn by George Klein in a more realistic style,

101. Venus and Sun Girl in an advertisement from *Miss America* after it had been transformed from a comic book into a magazine for girls. Obviously, Marvel intended these superheroines to appeal to female readers. (*Miss America Magazine* vol. 7, no. 12, July 1948.)

102. Of the four Marvel superheroines created between 1946 and 1948, Venus, the Most Beautiful Girl in the World, had the longest-lasting comic, which ran for a total of twenty-two issues. Ed Winiarsky, who drew this story, was the chief staff artist at Marvel in the early 1940s. (*Venus* no. 1, August 1948.)

103. The lineup in *Venus* included Hedy De Vine, a teen character whose own book had begun the year before; this feature also was drawn by Ed Winiarsky. (*Venus* no. 1, August 1948.)

and each comic book also included a "True-to-Life Romance" like "Leave Me Never" and "Without Love." Then the comic book acquired science fiction elements. Venus went to the moon and to the bottom of the ocean. She battled mad scientists in stories titled "The End of the World" and "Beyond the Third Dimension," and the backup stories, like "The Strange Rocket," now had science fiction themes.

Finally Bill Everett, creator of Sub-mariner and Namora, took over both the writing and drawing of the book from issue no. 14 until its last issue in 1952. He gave Venus a horror theme, and the subtitle changed from *Romantic Tales of Fantasy* to *Strange Stories of the Supernatural.*

104. Bill Everett took over the writing and drawing of Venus from issues no. 13 to no. 19, the final one. In these wordy panels, Everett returns to his favorite subject–sea creatures–and has Venus battling Neptuna, mistress of the sea. (*Venus* no. 18, 1952.)

105. Switched at birth? Bill Everett gave his issues of *Venus* a horror theme, and the comic's subtitle was changed from *Romantic Tales of Fantasy* to *Strange Stories of the Supernatural.* Among the ghosts and monsters that populated these later books was this sea creature from the final issue. (*Venus* no. 19, 1952.)

106. Remarkably similar is Gilbert Shelton's Phineas Freak, one of three hippies who starred in one of the most popular and durable underground comics. (*Fabulous Furry Freak Brothers,* 1980.)

Bill Everett's art, as always, was magnificent. He excelled at drawing beautiful women, an important requisite for illustrating "the most beautiful girl in the world," as Venus was billed. But his stories got weirder and wordier. Sometimes the speech balloons, lettered by Everett himself, took up half the panel. And by this time the theme of Venus as goddess of love come down to Earth, was almost completely obscured by the theme of monsters and ghosts. Although Everett did occasionally acknowledge that Venus was an immortal deity, most of the time he wrote and drew her as an editor covering news stories for *Beauty Magazine* who, as Whitney Hammond puts it, is "always stumbling into weird and strange adventures!" "Strange" was putting it mildly. In issue no. 19, the last issue of *Venus* comics, Everett confronted his heroine with a monster who bore an uncanny resemblance to cartoonist Gilbert

Shelton's Phineas Freak, of the underground comix classic *Fabulous Furry Freak Brothers.*

All four superheroines, along with Marvel's earlier superheroine, Miss America, were drawn in the same clear, accessible style used for the stories in Marvel's teenage girl titles. Venus, Blonde Phantom, Namora, and Sun Girl advertised in each other's books and in the girls' magazine, *Miss America.* Miss America herself shared Sun Girl's and Blonde Phantom's books. And Blonde Phantom appeared in Sun Girl and Namora. Venus featured guest appearances of teen comics heroine Hedy Devine, who obviously appealed to the same audience. It was a kind of superheroine slumber party.

Although Stan Lee attempted something similar in the seventies, this was the first time in the short history of comic books that an entire group of superheroines had been created specifically for girls.

Superman . . . I can't believe it. They're cheering me!

You deserve it, Supergirl! After all, you are the world's greatest heroine!

–conversation between Superman and Supergirl, *Action Comics* no. 285 (1962)

CHAPTER
7

The fifties were not a good time for costumed characters, male or female. Actually, the popularity of super-powered characters had been waning since the end of the war. Superhero comics, which had made up over ninety per cent of DC Comics' output during World War II, had been reduced to less than half of the line by 1949, and still further reduced to less than one-quarter of the line by the early 1950s. Possibly the American public had had enough of real violence after four years of war. Possibly there were simply no interesting villains left to fight. After fighting Nazi air aces and spies, real-life bank robbers seemed pretty tame.

By the 1950s, not only superhero books but the entire comic book industry was in a state of decline. The number of available comic book titles dropped from roughly 500 in 1952 to 300 in 1955. This sad state of affairs was partially due to the rise of a new medium: television. It was also due, in part, to a book called *Seduction of the Innocent*.

Seduction of the Innocent, published in 1954, was written by a psychiatrist named Dr. Fredric Wertham and purported to find a link between

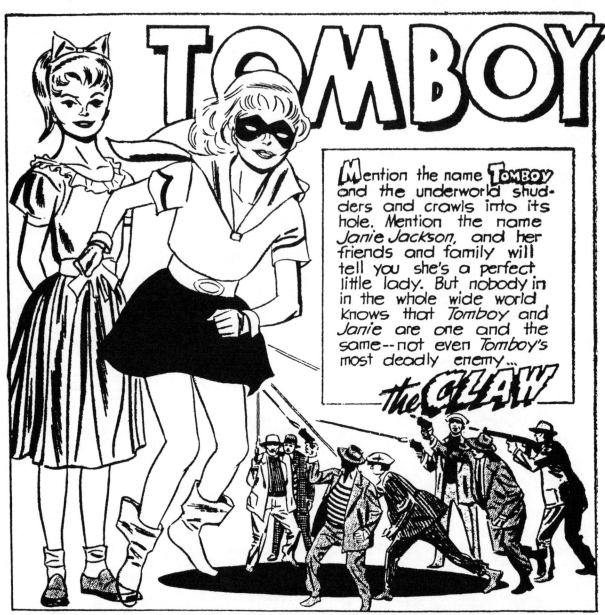

107. Although superhero comics declined precipitously in number in the 1950s and all the superheroines created during the 1940s disappeared, Marvel Comics introduced one new superheroine designed to appeal to female readers: Tomboy. Tomboy resembled Pauline Loth's Miss America in her graceful and acrobatic feats, though she packed a powerful punch as well. (*Captain Flash* no. 1, November 1954.)

108. Tomboy's secret identity was Janie Jackson, "a perfect little lady," the daughter of police lieutenant Charles Jackson. Readers were sure to identify with Janie/Tomboy when she was shown being teased by her older brother. He compared her unfavorably with Tomboy in a manner similar to the triangles involving adult superheroines, like Blonde Phantom, Mark Mason, and Louise Grant or Superman, Lois Lane, and Clark Kent. (*Captain Flash* no. 1, November 1954.)

reading comic books and juvenile delinquency. Whereas it was certainly true, as Wertham stated, that the vast majority of young criminals he studied were avid comic book readers, he neglected to mention that the vast majority of American children were avid comic book readers. And while some comics mentioned in Wertham's book were indeed objectionably violent, gruesome, and sadistic, he tended to get carried away and lump all action comics under the title "crime comics," including even *Wonder Woman*.

However faulty we may find Wertham's logic today, in 1954 his book had a powerful effect on an already paranoid American public, which soon added fear of the comic book menace to fear of the Red menace. A Senate subcommittee was formed to look into the dangers of comics, and in parts of America, concerned parents threw their children's favorite reading matter into bonfires. Most of the comic book publishers simply folded, leaving a diehard few, including Marvel and DC. This turn of events did not bode well for superheroines.

Some of the superwomen of the forties managed to struggle along into the first part of the fifties. Black Canary, appearing in *All Star*

109. When Janie becomes Tomboy, "the underworld shudders and crawls into its hole." Because of the hostile publishing climate of the 1950s, this charming character appeared in only three issues of the comic book headlined by the forgettable Captain Flash, and died with that book. (*Captain Flash* no. 1, November 1954.)

Comics, made it to 1951; Venus lasted until 1952. Mary Marvel disappeared, along with her publisher, Fawcett Comics, in 1954. Namora had her last watery adventure in her cousin Submariner's comic in 1955. And in 1954, an obscure but lovable superheroine named Tomboy popped up in the pages of *Captain Flash* comics for a short year's stay.

Tomboy was drawn by Jack Kirby, who is better known to comic fans as the creator of dozens of superheroes over a period of more than forty

110. Unlike Captain Marvel, who had developed an entire family in the Fawcett comics of the 1940s, Superman had to wait until what is usually called the silver age (the late 1950s and 1960s) before other Kryptonians showed up on Earth; here he meets Supergirl for the first time. Artist Al Plastino (b. 1921), a DC veteran who specialized in Superman and Batman stories, drew her origin story. (*Action Comics* no. 252, May 1959; reprinted in *Action Comics* no. 334.)

111. Supergirl's origin story explained that she escaped from Krypton along with the entire city of Argo, which her scientist father Zor-El, Superman's uncle, had had covered with a dome to protect it when the planet exploded. Argo was destroyed by a meteor shower, but her father saved her by placing her in a rocket aimed at Earth where she wound up in the Midvale Orphanage under the name Linda Lee and wearing a brown wig as a disguise. (*Action Comics* no. 252, May 1959; reprinted in *Action Comics* no. 334.)

years. Like Mary Marvel, Tomboy was not a grown woman, but a twelve-year-old girl. There's something wonderful about the criminal underworld shuddering in fear of a little girl, but according to the comic, that is what they did. "Mention the name Tomboy and the underworld shudders . . ." reads the caption in the comic's first panel. "Mention the name Janie Jackson, and her friends and family will tell you she's a perfect little lady. But nobody in the whole wide world knows that Tomboy and Janie are one and the same." The cute little blonde in the black mask swings from ropes and leaps into action with the agility of the best superheroes, and packs the punch of a prizefighter. As Janie Jackson, daughter of police lieutenant Charles Jackson, she ties her hair up in a big bow, wears fluffy dresses, and gets teased by her big brother, who sneers, "Ahh—! What does she know except to play with a lot of dolls and ribbons?" When she hears that the master criminal called The Claw is on the loose, Janie exclaims, "Oooh! I'm going to my room and lock the door!" Her brother laughs at her, "Isn't that just like a girl?" Of course, he doesn't know that she's gone to her room to change into Tomboy and catch The Claw, a nasty customer who appears to have furry bear paws for hands.

Just as thousands of twelve-year-old girls fantasized about becoming Mary Marvel, it's easy to imagine those same girls, teased by the boys as being "just like a girl," wanting to become a superheroine like Tomboy. Tomboy was a charming but minor character. Only one important and long-lasting superheroine emerged from the 1950s: Supergirl.

That Supergirl actually originated at all in 1959 is a minor miracle. By 1953, only the strongest supercharacters—Green Arrow, Aquaman, Superman, Batman, and Wonder Woman—were left at DC Comics. In 1956, DC editor Julius Schwartz tried to revive some of the more minor costumed heroes such as the Flash and Green Lantern in an anthology title called *Showcase,* but the real superhero revival was not to come about until the sixties. In the

112. DC's *Adventure Comics* is an anthology book that has launched many superheroes, from Superman to Streaky, the Super Cat, to Supergirl. She was created by editor Mort Weisinger and writer Otto Binder to star in a new *Action* backup feature, and after her origin story, Jim Mooney became the regular artist. Supergirl was prepared in secret by Superman for her role as a superhero, and her existence was revealed to the world in this 1962 story where she meets President and Mrs. Kennedy. (*Action Comics* no. 285, 1962.)

midst of this period, when comic books could only be described as an ailing medium, a small rocket ship from the domed Kryptonian city of Argo, bearing Superman's teenage cousin, Kara Zor-El, landed in *Action Comics* no. 252.

Superman's familiar origin had been simple: as the planet Krypton blows up, a scientist named Jor-El sends his baby son to Earth in a rocket. The baby is adopted by the couple who find him, and grows up to discover that he has super powers. Supergirl's origin was much more convoluted. Scientist Zor-El (Jor-El's brother),

upon discovering that Krypton is about to explode, encases his hometown, Argo City, in a dome. The inhabitants whirl through space, protected by their dome above and by ground covered with lead sheeting below, which keep away harmful radiation. Eventually a meteor shower smashes holes in the protective lead shield and, as the hapless citizens of Argo City drop like flies from radiation poisoning, Zor-El puts his teenage daughter, Kara, in an escape rocket aimed at Earth. Kara winds up in the Midvale orphanage, disguised by a brown wig, calling herself Linda

Lee, and secretly performing superfeats. Meanwhile, Kara's parents, who weren't killed after all, take refuge in a different dimension called the "survival zone," and eventually wind up living in Kandor, the city in a bottle that Superman keeps in his Fortress of Solitude.

Somehow, Supergirl manages to keep her existence a secret until 1962, by which time she has acquired a set of foster parents, Mr. and Mrs. Danvers, and the usual clueless boyfriend, Dick Malverne. Then, in a special issue of *Action Comics,* Superman introduces his cousin to the world. People react in various ways to the announcement of a new superheroine. A teenage girl thinks, "She's adorable! I *love* her

114. Streaky and Comet, the Superhorse, were both designed by Jim Mooney, who became the permanent Supergirl artist from her second appearance until 1968. Comet first appeared in *Action* no. 293. In one memorable story, he is transformed into a human being by the sorceress, Circe, and declares his love for Supergirl, a fantasy with undeniable appeal to young girls. (*Action Comics* no. 311, 1964.)

113. In the golden age of comics, humor and fantasy, incorporating animal sidekicks like Tawny the Talking Tiger, were specialties of the Fawcett Marvel Family titles. When superheroes took off again in the 1960s, DC introduced elements of fantasy reminiscent of the Fawcett comics, including superpets like Streaky, the Super Cat. Art by Mike Sekowsky and Jack Abel. (*Adventure Comics* no. 400, 1970.)

hair!" while a movie star thinks, "I'm Hollywood's most beautiful actress! But she'll attract more attention than me! . . . *Bah!*" And in Russia, Nikita Kruschev thinks, "(Groan) How can this snip of a child be mightier than all the Soviet atomic bombs put together? It must be a capitalistic *hoax!*"

The invincible teenager even meets President Kennedy, who tells her, "Supergirl, I know you'll use your superpowers not only to fight crime, but to preserve peace in our troubled world!"

Except for her first story, which was drawn by Al Plastino, Supergirl was drawn for the next nine years by Jim Mooney, who had drawn Wildfire eighteen years before. Her adventures were chronicled by a number of different writers, including Superman creator Jerry Seigel, science fiction writer Edmond Hamilton, and that wizard with superheroines, Otto Binder. Binder's hand can be seen in the gentle stories, with their elements of fantasy which are often reminiscent of his earlier super-powered teenager, Mary Marvel. In fact, Jim Mooney remembered that sometimes the stories were too gentle. He grew tired of drawing, in story after story, pictures of Supergirl rescuing busloads of orphans!

Supergirl was very clearly intended for young girls, and her stories contained all the right elements. She acquired a super-powered cat named Streaky and, best of all, a beautiful, telepathic white superhorse, Comet, both designed by Mooney. A 1964 Supergirl story, called "The Day Super-Horse Became Human," must have catered to the fantasies of thousands of horse-loving girls throughout America. In it, Comet, who has always secretly been in love with Supergirl, travels back through time and gets the sorceress, Circe, to transform him into a handsome young man called Bronco Bill. Through a series of bizarre coincidences, he winds up in the American West, wearing the discarded clothing of a bandit known as the Hooded Demon. He runs into Supergirl, who, in her disguise as Linda Lee, just happens to be on a field trip with her Midvale high school class. She falls in love with him, but when he is accused of being the Hooded Demon and Supergirl doesn't believe in his innocence, Bronco Bill has to become a horse again. In the end, the real Hooded Demon is caught and a remorseful Supergirl confides to her horse, "Oh, Comet! 'Bronco Bill' was so handsome . . . so noble! Why didn't I trust him! Now I'll probably never see him again!" And a lovelorn Comet thinks, "Fate plays strange tricks, Supergirl! Who knows! Some day you may meet this 'Bronco Bill' once more!"

Not only Supergirl, but most of the DC super-hero comics, had become extremely convoluted by the early 1960s. Superman, who originally had only green kryptonite to worry about (it took away his powers) now had a veritable rainbow of kryptonite to deal with, and each color had its own special effect on him. The favorite of writers who had run out of plot ideas must have been red kryptonite. Superman and Supergirl reacted differently each time they were exposed to it—a concept that offered endless possibilities.

Wonder Woman was also no longer the Amazon princess whom her fans from the forties had known and loved. Robert Kanigher had been writing her adventures since the death of William Moulton Marston in 1947 and, by 1960, he had added an entire Wonder family—Wonder Tot and Wonder Girl—to the comic, blissfully

115. Like Superman, Wonder Woman also was given a sort of family by DC writers and editors in the 1960s. Constraints imposed by the Amazon's origin story (she is the only child of Queen Hippolyta of Paradise Island) were overcome in a variety of imaginative ways. In "Wonder Girl Meets Wonder Woman," written by Robert Kanigher, Amazon scientists create a "miniature time-and-space projector" that allows Wonder Girl (Wonder Woman as a teenager) to meet her future self. Art by Ross Andru and Mike Esposito. (*Wonder Woman* no. 117, October 1960.)

ignoring the fact that they contradicted Wonder Woman's origin story as written by Marston. At first, stories with Wonder Tot (Wonder Woman as a baby) or Wonder Girl (Wonder Woman as a young girl) took place in the Amazon's past, but by 1963, Kanigher had abandoned all pretense at logic, and all three Wonder characters were appearing together in the same stories.

In a phone interview, this is how he rationalized having Wonder Woman and her past selves together in the same place at the same time: "Since I know nothing at all about science, what I did was have Hippolyta take slides, as a mother would, of her daughter as she grew up, and then by multiplex cinematography, she merges the pictures so they come to life at the same time."

The plausibility of this explanation did not seem to matter to fans of the book. A 1963 Wonder Woman letters page printed touching letters from girls who wanted to believe that their heroine was real, and who were inspired by her. Linda Parson wrote, "When another reader begged you to take her to Paradise Island, you answered that Paradise Island is imaginary. Well, how about taking me on an imaginary trip there?"

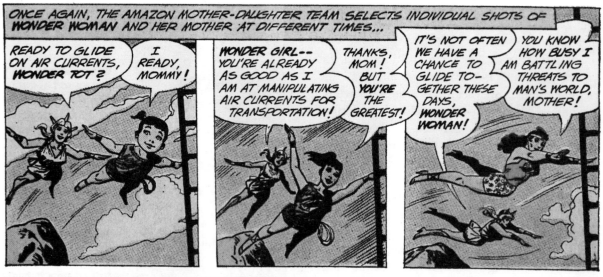

116. Because "impossible does not exist in the Amazon dictionary," writer Kanigher eventually united Wonder Woman with two younger versions of herself. Here is the entire Wonder family: Wonder Tot, Wonder Girl, Wonder Woman, and mom Hippolyta in the story, "The Return of Multiple Man." Art by Ross Andru and Mike Esposito. (*Wonder Woman* no. 129, April 1962.)

A letter from Melody Ann Salaun said something similar: "I'm only a little girl now, and my mother wouldn't let me come to visit you. But when I am 20, I intend to realize my life's ambition to visit you." Beryl Elaine Edwards wrote, "My sisters and I are your most loyal fans. . . And we try to do extra good work in school, because we know you would want us to."

Meanwhile, Marvel (then called Atlas Comics) had fared even worse than DC through-

out the fifties. By 1957, when they discontinued some fifty-five titles, superheroines had been long gone from the pages of their comic books. Editor Stan Lee had to let his entire staff of artists and writers go. All alone in his tiny office, he spent the next few years putting out a handful of comics filled with stories left over from the canceled books. When the superheroine finally returned to Marvel Comics in 1961, she would be literally invisible.

nvisible superheroines were nothing new to comics. In 1944, Ghost Woman was invisible to all except the arcane creatures of the night. But of course, she was already dead. Invisible Scarlet O'Neil, on the other hand, was extremely visible in American newspapers for fifteen years. Superheroines were comparatively rare in newspaper comic strips and Scarlet was one of perhaps three, the other two being Tarpe Mills's

117. Invisible Scarlet O'Neil was drawn only in outlines through which the background could be seen when she was using her ability to become invisible. (*Invisible Scarlet O'Neil*, Whitman Publishing Co., 1943.)

Miss Fury and Jack Sparling's Claire Voyant. The latter might or might not be considered a superheroine strip. Claire, as her name implies, possessed the ability to see into the future, but after her initial appearance in 1943, she seldom made use of this super power; the strip became a combination of adventure and soap opera.

Scarlet, however, continuously used her unique ability to render herself invisible by pressing a nerve on her left wrist. When this happened, artist Russell Stamm drew her with a

dotted line, so the reader knew she was there even if none of the strip's inhabitants could see her. Unlike so many other superheroines, the invisible woman didn't work for a detective—she was a detective. And her boyfriend Sandy, brighter than the average comic strip boyfriend, knew about her invisible alter ego for a change. From 1940 through 1955, Scarlet successfully fought gangsters, homicidal maniacs, and all other manner of unsavory characters. Like Miss Fury, her Sunday strips were repasted into comic book form and, in 1943, she was novelized in a book published by Whitman Publishing Company. She was a strong and competent female role model.

Sue Storm, aka Invisible Girl of the Fantastic Four, was another matter entirely. Creators Jack Kirby and Stan Lee came up with the idea for Marvel's first superhero team in 1961, after learning that DC was having considerable success in the shrunken comic market with their new superhero team book, *Justice League of America.* Marvel's answer to the Justice League consisted of three men—Reed Richards, Ben Grimm, and Johnny Storm—and Johnny's sister, Susan. When cosmic rays bombarded their experimental spacecraft, they each gained a special super power. Reed Richards became Mister Fantastic, gaining the Plastic Man–like ability to limitlessly stretch every part of his body, Johnny Storm became a new Human Torch, and Ben Grimm turned into the rocklike, powerful Thing. Although later Susan Storm gained the ability to project limited force fields, at first her only super power was that of invisibility. And she was indeed invisible, in more ways than one. The Invisible Girl was as wimpy as the weakest of comic book sidekicks. Even projecting the force field was often too much for her, and she had a habit of fainting, becoming hysterical, or bursting into tears. In a 1963 two-page spread called "Questions and Answers about the Fantastic Four," the Invisible Girl's hobbies are listed as: "Fashion, cooking, cosmetics and reading romantic novels." In the 1962 *Fantastic Four* no. 11 the supergroup receives fan mail and Sue is reduced to tears. "A number of readers have said that I don't contribute enough to you . . . you'd be—better off without me!" Reed Richards, Sue's fiancé, angrily announces, "Well, it's time to set the record straight—," and goes on

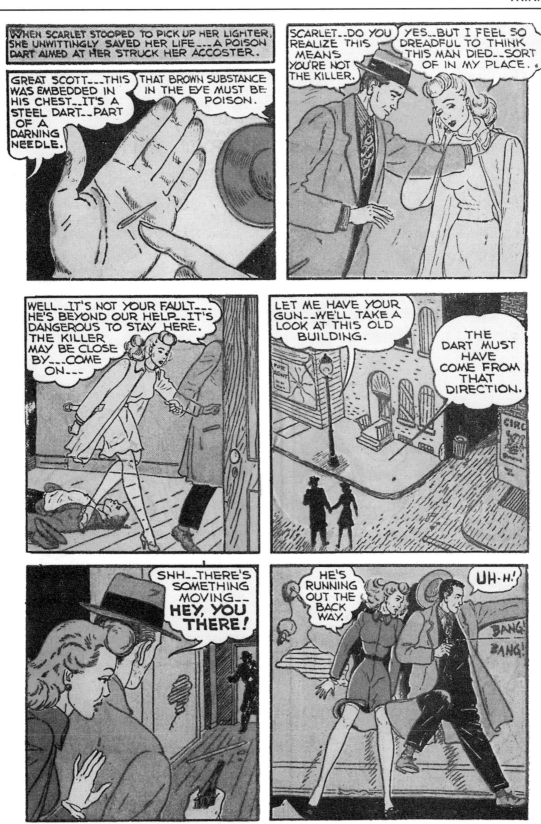

118. Three superheroines can be identified as having originated in newspaper comic strips: Miss Fury, Claire Voyant, and Invisible Scarlet O'Neil. Scarlet's scientist father inadvertently exposed her to an experimental ray in his laboratory which gave her the power to become invisible. Her strip was drawn and written by Russell Stamm, a former assistant to Chester Gould on *Dick Tracy*, and was repasted into comic book-page format for publication in *Famous Funnies* and three issues of her own book (1950–51). (*Famous Funnies*, 1947.)

119. Invisible Scarlet O'Neil investigates the criminal activities of Mr. Malignant. (*Invisible Scarlet O'Neil* no. 3, April 1951).

to justify the Invisible Girl by explaining how important Abraham Lincoln's mother was to him.

Within two years, Marvel's first supergroup had become so successful that the team of Stan Lee and Jack Kirby added two more supergroups to Marvel Comics' lineup. Both groups followed the formula of a bunch of guys and one girl.

Cartoonist Phil Yeh has said that if there is any message in the Marvel Comics of the sixties, it is that radiation is good for you. Cosmic rays created the Fantastic Four. The mighty green Hulk got that way by being bombarded with gamma rays. And Spider-Man was bitten by a radioactive spider. The X-Men are a supergroup composed of teenage mutants under the tutelage of mutant Professor Xavier. Xavier was born a mutant because his parents worked on early atomic experiments, and it is assumed that atomic energy also caused the strange powers of his students. If three guys and a girl had worked out so well in the Fantastic Four, Lee and Kirby must have reasoned, four guys and a girl would work even better. Cyclops wore dark glasses to shield his eyes, which emitted dangerously powerful

The Driver Gaped in Astonishment

121. In the 1940s, Whitman published a series of "mystery and adventure stories for girls and boys," licensed illustrated books based on comic strips, including *Brenda Starr* and *Tillie the Toiler,* or on Hollywood stars, including Deanna Durbin and Jane Withers. No. 2382 was *Invisible Scarlet O'Neil,* with twenty-one illustrations "adapted from the newspaper strip," but probably not by Russell Stamm. (*Invisible Scarlet O'Neil,* Whitman Publishing Co., 1943.)

120. Claire Voyant, a strip syndicated by New York's erudite and liberal *PM* newspaper between 1943 and 1948, was the creation of Jack Sparling (b. 1916), an unusual artist who drew both strips and comic book stories throughout his long career. He drew Fawcett's *Nyoka, the Jungle Girl* simultaneously with *Claire Voyant.* As with *Miss Fury* and *Scarlett O'Neill,* there were a few issues of a *Claire Voyant* comic and a couple of appearances in anthology books. (*Claire Voyant* no. 4, 1947, collecting strips from 1945–46.)

rays; the Angel had wings; Iceman was the Human Torch's opposite; and the Beast was a kind of flesh-and-blood Thing. And Jean Grey—Marvel Girl—possessed telekinetic powers. Like the Invisible Girl, her powers were limited; she tended to faint if she tried to telekinetically move something that was too big.

Actually, most of the women in Marvel's early supergroups possessed telekinetic powers of one kind or another. Jean Grey's ability to project force fields was a form of telekinesis, as was the "hex power" of the Scarlet Witch, the token woman member of a supergroup composed of evil mutants which opposed the X-Men. It was never explained why the ratio of male mutants to female mutants always seemed to be roughly four to one.

122. Sue Storm, the Invisible Girl, serves the coffee, goes to a fashion show, and faints. In the Fantastic Four, the first of a series of superhero groups created by writer-editor Stan Lee and artist-writer Jack Kirby for Marvel Comics at the beginning of the 1960s, each member of the group had character flaws, an element key to the success of Marvel characters like Spider-Man in the silver age of comic books (1956-1972). Unlike the insecurities and self-doubts that afflicted male heroes, and which encouraged the reader's identification and evoked admiration when the heroes overcame them, Sue Storm's power and flaws were almost a caricature of Victorian notions of the feminine, an invisible woman who faints when she tries to exert herself. (Top, bottom right: *Fantastic Four King-Size Special* no. 4, November 1966.)

123. Jean Grey serves dinner, and feels faint. The first incarnation of the X-Men, a supergroup of teenage mutants created by Lee and Kirby in 1963, included four men and one woman, Marvel Girl. While the male heroes of the Marvel supergroups blasted powerful rays from their eyes, burned or froze opponents, or threw powerful roundhouse punches, Marvel Girl and Invisible Girl had telekinetic rather than physical super powers and often demonstrated weakness rather than strength when they tried to use their gifts. (Left: *X-Men: The Early Years* no. 17, September 1995; right: *X-Men: The Early Years* no. 2, June 1994.)

124. Jean Grey versus the Scarlet Witch, who with her brother, Quicksilver, was a member of a supergroup of young mutants led by the evil mastermind, Magneto. Apparently Lee and Kirby saw no contradiction in introducing a scarlet woman character with the magical power to hex others into the pseudo-science fictional world of X-Men. The Scarlet Witch and Quicksilver soon saw the error of their ways and joined the Avengers. Art by Jack Kirby. (*X-Men* no. 11, 1965.)

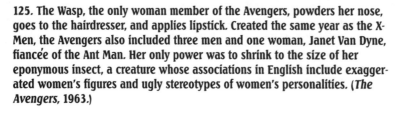

125. The Wasp, the only woman member of the Avengers, powders her nose, goes to the hairdresser, and applies lipstick. Created the same year as the X-Men, the Avengers also included three men and one woman, Janet Van Dyne, fiancée of the Ant Man. Her only power was to shrink to the size of her eponymous insect, a creature whose associations in English include exaggerated women's figures and ugly stereotypes of women's personalities. (*The Avengers*, 1963.)

Wanda the Scarlet Witch and her brother, Quicksilver, were both so very good-looking that it wasn't hard for the reader to guess they'd soon forsake their evil ways and join the good guys. They did, indeed, eventually become members of the Avengers, the other supergroup that started in 1963.

The Avengers consisted of, naturally, four guys and a girl. In this case, three of the guys—the Hulk, Thor, and Iron Man—each also had their own books. The fourth was Ant Man, who used a special serum to shrink, later discovering he also could use it to grow and become Giant Man. The girl was his fiancée, Janet Van Dyne, aka The Wasp. She never had her own book and she couldn't grow to giant proportions if her life depended on it; her only talent was to become the teeny-weeny Wasp. If any superheroine was wimpier than the Invisible Girl, it was the Wasp. About the only way she could help the Avengers fight villains was to fly around the enemy and distract him, so one of the more powerful members of her superteam could land a blow. She also went shopping a lot, as did Jean Grey and Susan Storm.

The age of the supergroups had arrived, and women had a very minor role in it. In contrast to the all-girl letter page from the 1963 *Wonder Woman*, a 1965 *Avengers* letter page was all-male, and included an angry letter from John Halloran of Indianapolis, Indiana, who complained about a recent letter which had criticized Captain America. "The thing that made me maddest," he wrote, "was that it was a girl doing all the griping." He went on to suggest that the girl readers stick to Millie the Model and Patsy Walker. Obviously, the age of all-boy comic fandom also had begun.

Printed on that same letters page was "The Mighty Marvel Checklist," subtitled "A Line-up Of Some Of The Marvel-ous Mags On Sale Right Now!" Half the titles listed are solo superhero books; the others are supergroups and two horror/science fiction titles. There are no solo superheroine books listed.

Meanwhile, back at DC Comics, Wonder Woman remained the only superheroine with her own book and, by 1965, she was going through radical changes. With issue no. 156,

writer-editor Robert Kanigher decided to bring the Amazon princess back to what was now being called the "golden age" of comics—the forties—and, basically, start all over again. He retold her origin story as written by William Moulton Marston. Penciler Ross Andru and inker Mike Esposito, who had been drawing the book all along, suddenly altered their styles to more closely resemble the art nouveau look of Harry G. Peter. The result was an interesting but faulty experiment, which came off as satire or high camp rather than as a tribute to the golden-age of comics. Although Kanigher revived such early characters as the Cheetah and Doctor Psycho, gone was the feeling of fantasy that had been found in Marston's stories. Gone were the mystic lost kingdoms, the fairy maidens of Venus, the land of the leprechauns.

Gone, also, was Wonder Tot, but not Wonder Girl. With a few years added to her age, and a few

126. The new "old" Wonder Woman. *Wonder Woman* was the only superheroine comic book to be continuously published through the 1950s collapse of the superhero market and into the revival of costumed characters in the 1960s. In 1965, DC writer and editor Robert Kanigher tried to recapture the feeling of the 1940s incarnation of the character. Artists Ross Andru and Mike Esposito began to draw her stories in a style like that used by Harry G. Peter. (*Wonder Woman* no. 163, July 1966.)

127. Marvel's multiplying supergroups of the 1960s led their DC rivals to increase their own roster of superhero societies, and in 1964 three young male sidekicks of superheroes, Robin, Kid Flash, and Aqualad, were joined to a new version of Wonder Girl to form the Teen Titans. (*Teen Titans* no. 22, 1969.)

128. The new "new" Wonder Woman, at the opening of Diana Prince's English mod–influenced boutique. In 1968, writer Denny O'Neil and artists Mike Sekowsky and Dick Giordano created a Wonder Woman who was more Emma Peel than Amazon princess, who dressed in Carnaby Street fashions and studied martial arts under a wise and aged mentor named I Ching, after the Chinese divinatory book that was suddenly being bought and revered by every would-be hip teenager in the United States. (*Wonder Woman*, 1968.)

inches to her bustline, she was now part of a teenage supergroup that started in 1966 and included Batman's young sidekick, Robin, and teenage versions of Aquaman (Aqualad) and the Flash (Kid Flash). Naturally, Wonder Girl was the only female member of the group.

For Wonder Woman, the situation was to get worse before it got better. In 1968, she gained a new creative team and lost everything else—her Amazon powers, her costume, and Paradise Island, along with all her sister Amazons, who disappeared into another dimension. Steve Trevor was even killed off. In stories written by Denny O'Neil and drawn by Mike Sekowsky and Dick Giordano, she acquired a mentor—an ancient, blind martial arts master named I Ching—and a new mod wardrobe. She opened a boutique! And for the next four years, clad in

129. While Wonder Woman was exploring Asian religion and English fashion, Batgirl continued to appear with her male mentor and his teen sidekick in *Batman*, *Brave and Bold*, and *Detective Comics*. The Batgirl of the 1960s was also depicted as being concerned with her looks, as in this story where she is distracted from crime fighting by a run in her tights. Art by Gil Kane and Sid Green. (*Detective Comics*, 1968.)

white outfits obviously inspired by the sixties British television show, *The Avengers*, the New Wonder Woman, as she was billed, used only karate to fight off the bad guys.

Letters to the *Teen Titans* show that readers were already hopelessly confused about how Wonder Girl and Wonder Woman could exist together at the same time. Deborah Carey, of Cibolo, Texas, wrote, "How can Wonder Woman appear as both Wonder Girl in the *Teen Titans* and Wonder Woman in the *JLA [Justice League of America]*? This should cause a time paradox or at least a bit of confusion when both groups get together." By 1969, the readers had a new problem with the logic, or lack thereof, in the stories: if all the Amazons had gone off to another dimension, what was Wonder Girl still doing there? Or, as Daerick Gross, of Kettering, Ohio, put it, "Where does that leave Wonder Girl? Non-existent!"

Writer Marv Wolfman solved the problem by giving Wonder Girl a new origin and a new identity. She wasn't an Amazon after all. Instead, as a two-year-old baby she had been rescued

from a burning building by Wonder Woman, brought to Paradise Island, and adopted by Queen Hippolyta. Wonder Girl was now a whole new superheroine.

The Teen Titans seemed to be one book that still had a female readership. Most of the letter pages included at least one letter from a girl. (Sue Smith, of Stow, Ohio, wrote in 1969: "Please put another girl in the TT. It'd give WG someone to talk to.")

"Batgirl's Costume Cut-ups!," a 1968 story in *Detective Comics,* best illustrates the then-prevailing attitude toward superheroines. A caption on the first page gives us the story's theme: "Even *Batgirl* during her most hectic moments—when she is battling criminals—is always conscious of her appearance!" Barbara Gordon, alias Batgirl, is fighting a gang of robbers, when her headpiece gets knocked off-center. "As any girl will . . . " says the caption, she straightens the headpiece out, leaving herself open for a kick from one of the crooks. She thinks, "Ohhh—serves me right for being more concerned with my appearance

130. Invisible Scarlet O'Neil takes care of a crook. (*Invisible Scarlet O'Neil* no. 3, April 1951).

than those *Radball Robbers* . . ." Batman and Robin show up to catch the bad guys, and Batgirl complains to them, "My vanity betrayed me!"

The next day, determined to make up for that pesky "instinctive female reaction" by fighting crime, she follows Batman and Robin to the scene of a robbery at a sawmill, where they are having it out with the robbers while balancing on floating logs. Just like a girl, her "reaction to seeing Batman and Robin in danger" is "to let one go from [her] vocal chords!" Her scream distracts the "Dynamic Duo," who then get knocked off the logs. Robin says, "Even such determined fighters as we are—get distracted by a lady's scream!"

"It's up to me to stop those crooks now!" says Batgirl, chasing the bad guys. One of the robbers throws a log at her. It misses, but she gets splattered with mud, and again her vanity betrays her. "In reflex action, her gloved hand lifts to her face—" to wipe off the mud and, of course, the crooks get away.

Finally, Batgirl gets another chance at catching the robbers, when they strike at an outdoor charity ball. Batman and Robin are badly outnumbered, nine to two. Robin calls to Batgirl, "*Help us!* We've got a problem!" Batgirl extends "her shapely leg" and answers, "I have a bigger one—*a run in my tights!*" Suddenly the nine bad guys pause in the act of punching out Batman and Robin, to stare at her leg. "Lawbreaker eyes stare admiringly," reads the caption. "What a pair of gams!" exclaims a robber, and they actually whistle! "Taking advantage of the leggy diversion," Batman and Robin mop up the crooks. Robin comments, "*Batgirl's* femininity gave us a break this time!"

Wonder Woman was running a boutique. Batgirl was applying lipstick while Batman and Robin fought for their lives. The sixties was such a low point for superheroines that there was nowhere to go but up. And, in the seventies, things did improve.

All right girls, that finishes off these male chauvinist pigs! From now on, it's the Valkyrie and her lady liberators!

–Valkyrie to the women members of the Avengers, *The Avengers* no. 83 (1970)

CHAPTER **9**

In 1970, Marvel's *The Avengers* featured a story, written by Roy Thomas and drawn by John Buscema, titled "Come On In . . . The Revolution's Fine." On the first page, Janet Van Dyne, aka the Wasp, returning to the Avengers' mansion after visiting a sick aunt, finds a meeting taking place between the female team members—the Scarlet Witch, the Black Widow, and Medusa—and a strange platinum blonde named Valkyrie. In response to the Wasp's question: "Why are you all gathered here—in *Avenger's mansion?*" Scarlet Witch answers, "This is *our* mansion, our head-quarters for we are—*The Liberators!*" Informing

131. Valkyrie discovers that she has super powers and decides to use them to seek revenge on sexist men in a flashback sequence from Marvel's *The Avengers.* (*The Avengers* no. 83, December 1970.)

the Wasp that soon she will lose "the invisible *shackles* which men have placed on you!" the Valkyrie relates her origin. In a flashback sequence, we see her as a struggling chemistry student, ignored by her teacher who tells her, "I'm *busy,* young lady, *very* busy! If I find I need a secretary, I shall contact you!"

Angrily, the young student works late at the lab, muttering, "The old *fool*—the old *male* fool! He lives in a *dream-world* where *men* have all the brains . . . and *women* do all the work! Well, I'll *show* him . . . show them *all* . . . no matter how *late* I have to work . . . !"

"However," the caption tells us, "long hours and fatigue finally took their *toll* . . ." She collapses ("a smoking vial still clutched in my

outstretched hand . . .") and wakes to discover that she has "gained fantastic *strength!* Unbelievable *power!*" Lifting a car, she shouts, "*Male chauvinist pigs—beware! Beware—the Valkyrie!*"

Valkyrie convinces the other women to join her, and in the ensuing battle royal, as they beat the stuffing out of the male team members, Valkyrie shouts, "You have uttered your famous '*Avengers assemble*' for the *final* time! From now on, the war cry to *remember* shall be—*up against the wall, male chauvinist pigs!*" Disappointingly, Valkyrie turns out really to be the Enchantress, a supervillainess whose intention is the destruction of both sexes. "*All* of you have served your purpose . . . and so must *die* . . . ," she announces. But her magic is turned back upon her, and she vanishes. "She died the very death she planned for all of *us!*" says Black Widow, and Scarlet Witch answers, "*Did* she? I wonder . . . !?"

In the last panel, the Wasp and her tall boyfriend, Giant Man, are arguing. "You birds finally learned your lesson about that *women's lib* bull!" says the big guy. "That's what *you* think—*male chauvinist pig!*" shouts the tiny lady. "One of these days the *Liberators* will stage a comeback—"

Feminism, in a slightly addled form, had filtered into the Marvel Comics bullpen, and would stay there at least through the seventies.

Valkyrie herself, too good a character to toss away, returned, attitude and all, as a separate person from the Enchantress in 1972, and joined yet another Marvel superteam called the Defenders. On the cover of issue no. 4, astride a winged horse, she raises her spear and shouts, "Fellow Defenders! Your *foes* attack—and you *puny males* are too *weak* to stand against them! *But I can!*" The caption beneath this picture reads, "*Valkyrie Rides Again!*" But the platinum-haired fugitive from a Wagner opera has become just a little less radical. At the end of the story, in reply to Submariner's question, "It is said that you *hate* men. Why should *you* aid us?" she says, "I do *not* hate men, Submariner. I merely *know* I'm as *good* as they are."

The same year as the Valkyrie's unsuccessful takeover of the Avengers, Black Widow (who started out as a Soviet spy, but later joined the good guys) had an eight-issue run in the back of Marvel's *Amazing Adventures.* Among the various artists who worked on the eight stories were John Buscema and Bill Everett, both of whom

132. Marvel launched some short-lived titles featuring women heroes at the beginning of the 1970s, when this backer board for comic racks was produced. Jungle queen Shanna, the She-Devil (left), got her own book in December 1972 after several appearances in *Savage Tales,* and four issues of *The Cat* (right) appeared between November 1972 and June 1973.

133. Women's Liberation comes to Marvel. Led by the Valkyrie, the women members of the Avengers pound the guys into submission while spouting women's liberation slogans in the 1970 story, "Come on in . . . the Revolution's Fine." Valkyrie pretends that she had been a scientist, denigrated by her male colleagues because of her gender, and that she had gained her superpowers in a lab accident. At the end of the story, however, it is revealed that she is really the Enchantress. Thus, the feminist turns out to have been a witch. (*The Avengers* no. 83, December 1970.)

had also worked on Marvel's romance comics and who drew women in a sensitive and decorative style that appealed to a female audience.

The start of the adventure finds Black Widow, as her alter ego Natasha Romanoff, living the life of a socialite with a penchant for European film directors. (In issue no. 1, she makes a date with "Guy Desmond . . . one of the biggest film directors in the *world!*" and in issue no. 2, she's kissing Roman Wilson, who tells her, "I hope you are *serious* . . . not because I am a famous *director* . . . but because you *care* for me . . .") Natasha gets bored with her life, and in no time has changed into her Black Widow outfit (a skintight black jumpsuit reminiscent of those worn by Miss Fury and Black Venus) and gotten involved with humanist causes like the "Young

Warriors," a group of Puerto Rican teenagers who take over a building in Spanish Harlem from a crooked slumlord and turn it into a center for underprivileged children.

A new generation had grown up since Venus ended her adventures in 1952, and their memories did not include any women superheroes outside the supergroups. Thus, in 1971, Shirley A. Gorman of Hereford, Texas, wrote to *Amazing Adventures:* "You might say that Madame Natasha is what women's lib is all about. . . . Until this new Black Widow came along Marvel never had a solo female star. You have great female characters but they are all part of the same group. Natasha is her own woman."

All comic genres seem to have a life span. Superhero comics had bloomed and died and come back to life again. The romance comic books, an enormous part of the market since the late forties, were breathing their last by the early seventies, taking with them what was left of the female audience. The huge college audience that had bought the *X-Men* and the *Fantastic Four* throughout the sixties was mostly male. And now, Stan Lee tried to reach a girls' market again by bringing superheroines back into comics. Lee, who had been responsible for the great superheroine girls' club of the late forties, was the right man for the job. During the sixties, he had tackled socially responsible subjects like ecology and racism. He had introduced several African American superheroes. And in 1972, he produced three comic books with female protagonists, all aimed at a female audience: a jungle adventure (*Shanna, the She-Devil*), an action-romance (*Night Nurse*), and a superheroine comic (*The Cat*).

The Cat used a woman writer, Linda Fite, who remembers: "Women's lib was in full tilt boogie at the time. Roy [Thomas] and Stan [Lee] were not always trendsetters, but they would see a trend and follow it." So, employing women to write and draw—Marie Severin drew the first two issues and Paty Greer drew issue no. 3—Marvel published their first superheroine book in twenty years. *The Cat* lasted only four issues; a fifth issue was penciled by Ramona Fradon, but never saw print. Nevertheless, what was left of the female readership took notice. In issue no. 3, Shira J. Rosan expressed the feelings of many other women when she wrote: "I have always felt the lack of, and . . . rather wistfully longed for a superhero with whom I could identify more completely than I have been able to with, say Sue Richards . . . or the Wasp: I was wishing for a smarty-pants, wise-cracking, strong, brave-coura-geous-and-bold, bounce-backable woman: and, in the Cat, I think I see the beginnings of her."

The Cat was the first of what would be over a decade of superheroines to emerge from the Marvel offices as stars of their own comics. At the beginning of 1973, Bill Everett, still writing and drawing Submariner, brought back Venus, whom he had drawn twenty years before. Sadly, that was the last issue of *Submariner* that he produced before his death, so we will never know where he would have taken his revived character or whether he could have convinced Stan Lee to give Venus back her own book.

134. Norse mythology had already provided Marvel with one successful character, the Mighty Thor, who first appeared in *Journey Into Mystery* in 1962. When superheroines were multiplying at Marvel in the early 1970s, Valkyrie must have seemed too good a character to abandon after one appearance, and she joined yet another Marvel superteam called the Avengers in 1972 in a story by Steve Englehart with art by Sal Buscema. (*Defenders* no. 4, 1972.)

135. Most of the superheroines created at Marvel in the 1960s were team players, but one of the most durable and interesting was a solo act. Natasha Romanov is a former Soviet spy who has joined the good guys and changes from international socialite with a penchant for European filmmakers to crime fighter when she dons her skintight black jumpsuit. (*Amazing Adventures* nos. 1 and 2, 1970.)

136. Natasha as Black Widow in action. She first appeared in 1964, but became more prominent in the 1970s when she teamed up with Daredevil and had a solo run in eight stories scripted by Gary Friedrich and drawn by John Buscema (as shown here) and Bill Everett. (*Amazing Adventures* no. 1, August 1970.)

1977 saw the debut of *Ms. Marvel*. Although everyone agrees that the new superheroine was thought up by Stan Lee, there's some question about who came up with her name. Gerry Conway, who wrote the first few issues, stated in issue no. 1 that Roy Thomas thought up the name. Roy Thomas insists it was Stan Lee, and Stan Lee doesn't remember.

Journalist Carol Danvers, Ms. Marvel's alter ego, also doesn't remember. Specifically, in the first few issues, she blacks out whenever her super powers take over, and wakes up later without any memory of what happened. In a full-page editorial, Gerry Conway explained this in feminist terms: ". . . You might see a parallel between her [Ms. Marvel's] quest for identity, and the modern woman's quest for raised consciousness, for self-liberation, for identity. . . . Ms. Marvel . . . is influenced, to a great extent, by

the move towards woman's liberation." Conway goes on to explain and apologize that the book is being written by a man rather than a woman: ". . . For whatever reason (right or wrong), at the moment there are no thoroughly trained and qualified women writers working in the super-hero comics field. . . . There should be, no denying it, but there aren't."

He was right. Women working in comics had hit an all-time low by the sixties and seventies. Still, the men at Marvel continued to plug away gamely, and in 1978 they came up with the Spider-Woman. Like Peter Parker, who became Spider-Man after being bitten by a radioactive spi-

AS THE FOG COMES, SANDBURG-LIKE, ON LITTLE CAT FEET--*THE CAT* PAUSES, PERPLEXED AT THE FEELINGS WHICH HAVE BROUGHT HER TO THE ROOFTOP OF THIS *CHICAGO HOSPITAL.*

WHY DO I SENSE THAT *DR. TUMOLO* HAS DRAWN ME HERE? WHEN I LEFT HER, ALL CRITICAL LIFE SIGNS WERE AT AN *END.*

COULD I HAVE BEEN *MISTAKEN?*

138. The Cat wore a skintight yellow jumpsuit and gloves outfitted with retractable metal claws that allowed her to scale buildings, while lenses in her hood provided enhanced night vision. Paty Greer penciled the third issue, with inks by Bill Everett. (*The Cat* no. 3, April 1973.)

ARE YOU *INJURED?*

ONLY MY *PRIDE!* I SHOULD'VE BEEN MORE *AWARE!*

137. A short-lived experiment in employing women creators was Marvel's *The Cat.* Aspiring scientist Greer Nelson was secretly given extraordinary mental and physical powers by her mentor, Dr. Joanne Tumolo, and went one-on-one with supervillains like Daredevil's foe, the Owl. Linda Fite was the writer for the entire series and Marie Severin drew the first two issues; on issue number two, she worked with Jim Mooney. (*The Cat* no. 2, January 1973.)

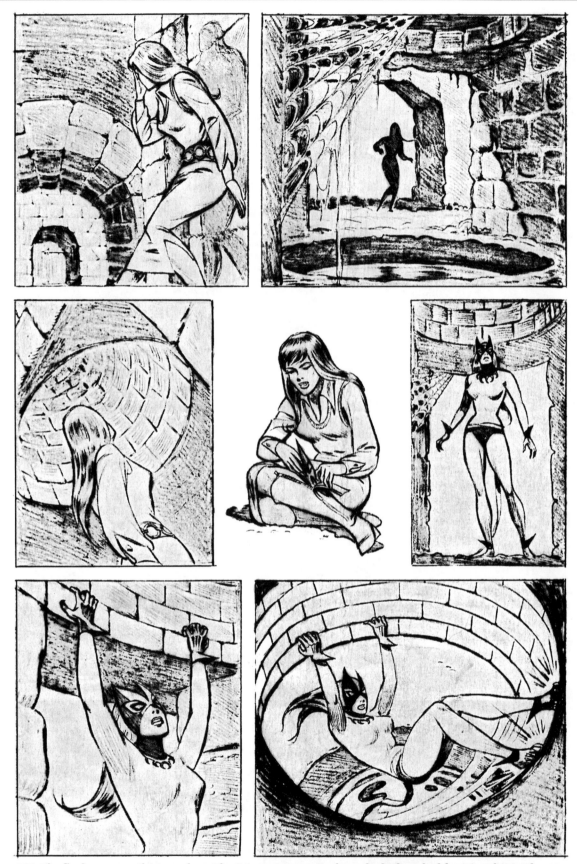

139. The final woman artist to work on *The Cat* was Ramona Fradon, who had worked for DC and Marvel since the early 1950s. She penciled issue no. 5 from Linda Fite's script, but the book was canceled before it was published and her pencils were never inked. (Collection of Ramon Fradon.)

Opens and runs for two more pages or so with Cat working out across
   town in new outfit, trying out new features, discussing why the
   changes were made (she never did like the other one all that much,
   Mal Donalbain designed it, etc.) Feeling real melancholy, lonely.
   Her only good friend, Dr. Tumolo, is a happy vegetable. A few city
   folk might look up and notice her, and suddenly she is being
   pursued by the police (ubiquitous in Chicago). This lasts for
   only a while, because they don't have the ability to scale walls--
   but they almost trap her, etc. Can go on for at least a page and ½.

Makes it back to her apartment--trying to figure out why the cops were
   so mean and ugly--shooting at her, etc. She's pretty rattled, cuz
   she thought all that had been cleared upweeks ago. Turns on TV
   to see if she can get any info--News broadcast reports that a
   West African (Angola) dignitary is missing, feared kidnapped.
   His car was found in ditch out in country and the chauffeur was
   mysteriously killed--claw marks ail over him--bled to death.
   Phone call from a Chicago Witch Cult links death and kidnapping
   to The Cat--(witch claims that the Cat is a sister of Satan, too--
   and is being compelled by him to do terrible stuff. Greer is
   furious, needless to say. There's an all-point-bulletin out on
   her. 'Armed and considered dangerous.'

Next out to this witch-lady's house*(I'll esplain how she got address
   etc. in caption or balloon). Witch named Miss Graymalkin opens
   her door--tall, very thin, angular, about 45, Lauren Bacallish?
   Greer has come on the pretext that she is writing a term paper
   on witchcraft or something. Gray shows her in--whol house is
   filled with cats--scores of 'em. Graymalkin charming, coldly--
   serves tea. Greer unwittingly drinks it--and it contains an
   odorless, tasteless drug/potion. Greer goes bananas--room spins,
   she sees wild colors, etc. (Special effects-type jaxx).
   Before she goes out completely has brief vision of being surrounded
   by a bunch of real witchy looking witches (Gray not among them).
   A flurry and flapping of hong sleeves and capes, and she is out.

Comes to only to find herself prisoner in an honest-to-god dungeon.
   Almost thinks she's still hallucinating when a processional of
   witches comes down the corridor, led by Graymalkin, now dressed
   in full regalia--fantastic costume. All witches carry candles,
   and they are followed and intermingled with all kinds of cats.
   The West African is bound. (RAMONA: A lot of explanation of
   purpose comes in here, so draw out this scene in several panet
   so I can get it all in, please.) Graymalkin says, in effect:
   "For centuries,innocents have been killed for our sins (ha ha),
   while we witches continued to hold sway over the masses, exacting
   tribute and running our own unique protection raquet. But people
   like this man weaken our hold, for most of our power comew from
   the superstition and fear of our bictims. This man, and others
   like him, educate teh people, dispel the fear and thereby destroy
   our livelihood." Graymalkin's world wide plan: take over the
   world as follows. "All these cats are the embodiments of the
   damned spirits of past witches. (ASIDE TO ANGOLIAN:'How do you
   think your chauffeur died, sir?' Dignitary probably has a thing
   or two to say in rebuttal) What we plan to do is inhabit your
   bodies with the essence of one of these cat-witches. We already
   have several of our sisters in high places--and they have seen
   to it that the populace is becoming increasingly afraid, and

140. Linda Fite had completed the script for *The Cat* no. 5 when the series was canceled; one page from the unpublished script is reproduced here.

der, Jessica Drew was injected with an irradiated spider serum which, the caption says, "changed her into the fearsome *dark angel of night.*" Marie Severin, who, along with Ramona Fradon, was the only major woman artist to emerge from comic books in the sixties, designed Spider-Woman's costume, and the superheroine with spider powers lasted five years.

That same year saw a single appearance of one of the most unusual superheroines to grace a comic book page. Flo Steinberg had come to work at Marvel as Stan Lee's girl Friday in 1963, at a time when the tiny Marvel staff consisted of her, production manager Sol Brodsky, and Lee, with Jack Kirby, who was freelancing, occasionally coming in to the office to pick up or drop off work. Fifteen years later, Marvel, now a flourishing company, published an oddball tribute to the comic book that had started them back on the road to success: *What If The Original Marvel Bullpen Had Become The Fantastic Four?* In this fanciful story, written and drawn by Kirby, "Fabulous Flo," as Stan Lee named her, became the Invisible Girl, a rare case of a real-life human being becoming a comic book character. As for the other fantastic three: Brodsky flamed on as the Torch, Stan Lee was Mister Fantastic, and Kirby himself became The Thing.

Mutants had definitely taken off at Marvel, and most of the new supercharacters created throughout the seventies were mutations of some kind or other. *X-Men,* the series that had started the mutant craze, was actually discontinued in 1970 because of low sales figures, but a revamped version, *The All-New, All-Different X-Men,* featuring a new team of mutants, was brought back in 1975, written by Len Wein and drawn by Dave Cockrum. Among the new characters introduced was Storm, a goddesslike figure from Africa who could control the weather. In fact, when we first meet her, Storm actually believes herself to be a goddess, as do the tribespeople who come to her during a famine, begging her to produce rain for them. Professor Xavier has to explain to her that she is really a mutant. Although she never had her own book, Storm, a beautiful African American woman with long white hair, became the leader of the X-Men and a major character in the world of Marvel comics.

By issue no. 96, Chris Claremont had taken over as writer of the *X-Men,* a position he would hold for the next seventeen years. One of the first alterations he made was to Jean Grey—Marvel Girl. Changed by cosmic forces into a character now called Phoenix, she wore a much more interesting costume and acquired stronger powers than any other Marvel heroine.

141. Bill Everett had played a key role in the creation of Marvel's superheroines aimed at female readers in the 1940s. When Marvel was creating more in the 1970s, he worked on *The Cat* and, in the last issue of *Sub-Mariner* that he drew before his death, reintroduced Venus, the most successful of the earlier generation of super-powered women. (*Sub-Mariner* no. 57, 1973.)

In 1977, the penciling and inking team of John Byrne and Terry Austin joined Claremont. Byrne and Claremont created new and interesting female team members, including thirteen-year-old Kitty Pryde, Marvel's first Jewish super-heroine, and Rogue, a bad girl turned good who had a Southern accent and a white streak in her hair. The new characters had distinct personalities; there had never before been a Jewish superheroine or one with a Southern accent. And, by slowly adding superheroines to the team, Claremont broke out of the old "three guys and a girl" formula of the sixties.

By 1980, Phoenix's powers had grown stronger than ever, and she ran amok. Eventually, in her newest persona as Dark Phoenix, she destroyed an entire solar system, including the inhabitants of one of its planets, a race of sentient beings who bore a strong resemblance to ambient asparagus stalks. For this she had to die, and die she did. In issue no. 137, the Dark Phoenix self-destructed, ensuring the continued popularity of *X-Men*. This was the first time that a major comic character actually died, but it would not be the last.

The success of *X-Men* spawned a host of new comics starring male and female mutant super-groups. The first of these, *The New Mutants,* created by Claremont in 1983, featured a multiracial, multinational group of teenage mutants, five of whom were girls: Wolfsbane, a girl werewolf from Scotland; Ilyana, a fifteen-year-old Russian; Magma, from a lost ancient Roman civilization; a Vietnamese boatperson named Karma; and a Native American teenager called Mirage. At this point, the ratio of super-powered girls to guys increased to fifty-fifty.

"X" titles proliferated, and eventually formed their own industry within Marvel comics: *X-Factor, X-Force, Excalibur, Generation X,* and *Generation NeXt.* Due in large part to Claremont's sympathetic handling and delineation of strong women characters, *X-Men* had the largest female readership of any Marvel comic.

Meanwhile, over at DC comics, although Wonder Woman and Supergirl were still gamely fighting the forces of evil, new superheroines were not exactly popping up like daffodils in spring. One hauntingly mystic character who did emerge from DC in 1973 was Black Orchid, who starred in *Adventure Comics* for all of three issues.

142. Ms. Marvel is "stronger than ten men, she can fly, and . . . she has an uncanny seventh sense which let's [*sic*] her anticipate an opponent's attack before it occurs," but all this still wasn't enough to keep her book going past its second year. Gerry Conway both wrote and edited the first few issues, and John Buscema was the artist for issue nos. 1–3. (*Ms. Marvel* no. 2, February 1977.)

Drawn in a decorative, almost psychedelic style by Tony De Zuniga, the ethereal Black Orchid was stronger than she looked; bullets bounced off her, and she flew through the air like an exotic purple bird. She was a master of deception, disguising herself as a different person in each adventure, but her true persona was to remain a mystery for almost twenty years.

143. Marvel's attempted sensitivity to women's issues didn't stop them from taking action in the 1970s against New York's Spider Woman Theater for using the name of their new superheroine. The women's theatrical group was, of course, named for the Native American goddess, while Marvel's creation was a female version of their popular Spider-Man. The art of Carmine Infantino appeared in many of the issues of the first year and a half of the book, and the cover above was reproduced from his and Steve Leialoha's original art. (*Spider-Woman* no. 7, 1978.)

By the early seventies, the women's movement had made its way into television as well as comics, and two popular television shows that were being avidly watched by American women and girls were *Wonder Woman* and *The Mighty Isis*. Since *Wonder Woman* was, of course, already a DC comic, it seemed natural for DC to turn the tables and produce a comic adaptation of *The Mighty Isis*, which they did in 1976, with art by Rick Estrada and Wally Wood. *The Mighty Isis* starred the Egyptian goddess herself as a super-

heroine. "Andrea Thomas . . . plain ordinary *science teacher*," the comic tells us, ". . . was part of an expedition searching for bygone civilizations . . ." Digging in the Egyptian desert, she uncovers "an *amulet* . . . and a *scroll!*" Something compels her to put the amulet on, and she gains the magical ability to read the hieroglyphs on the scroll. It tells her that she now has "the powers of the goddess Isis" and that, to activate those powers, "you must repeat the words *Mighty Isis!*" Wearing a nicely adapted 1976 version of an

144. Flo Steinberg as Invisible Girl, from *What if the Original Marvel Bullpen had become the Fantastic Four?*, written and drawn by Jack Kirby. The letter column of this issue notes that Roy Thomas conceived the idea of turning the Marvel Bullpen into the Fantastic Four (he had written himself and his wife Jeannie into the women's liberation story in *Avengers* no. 83). That's editor Stan Lee as Mister Fantastic on the left, Kirby as the Thing at center, and Sol Brodsky as the Human Torch on the right. (*What If?* no. 11, October 1978.)

145. In 1975, the *X-Men*, Marvel's original teenage mutant supergroup, underwent a makeover, incorporating a new cast of characters, including Storm, the first African American superheroine. This panel by Dave Cockrum is from the first issue of *X-Men* written by Chris Claremont. Storm, who came to the United States from Africa, had the power to control the weather and, in later issues, became the leader of the X-Men. (*X-Men* no. 96, 1975.)

"... FOR MORE THAN A SINGLE TERRAN LIFE HANGS IN THE BALANCE. LEFT UNCHECKED, THIS FORCE COULD THREATEN THE ENTIRE *COSMOS!* "

BUT EVEN AS THE SKY-RIDER OF THE SPACE-WAYS SPEEDS 'ROUND THE GLOBE -- EVEN AS OTHERS BECOME AWARE OF HER EXISTENCE --

--THE DARK PHOENIX BIDS FAREWELL TO HER HOMEWORLD...

... AND SOARS SPACEWARD TO FULFILL HER MALEFIC DESTINY.

146. Dark Phoenix, penciled by John Byrne and inked by Terry Austin. She's already suffering from lack of pupil, a disease that would afflict many future superheroines. Chris Claremont became the longest-serving writer on the *X-Men* series and, when he was joined by artist John Byrne, they opened an era of immense popularity for the mutant supergroup that saw the publication of a wide variety of *X-Men*–related titles and the addition of many other women characters. (*X-Men* no. 135, 1980.)

MIGHTY ISIS

147. In the 1970s, *Wonder Woman* was adapted for a live-action, prime-time television series, and soon was followed by an original TV production, *The Mighty Isis.* DC published seven *Isis* comic books; in this panel from issue no. 1, which was inked by Wally Wood, science teacher Andrea Thomas makes the switch to Mighty Isis. (*Isis* no. 1, November–December 1976.)

148. A decorative panel from the first Black Orchid story, drawn by Alex Niño and Tony De Zuniga. The first Earth Day was observed in 1970 and, in the next two years, DC created two superheroes born from the earth. Swamp Thing, inspired by the Heap from *Airboy* comics, rose from the bayous of Louisiana, and Black Orchid, a superheroine named for a flower, appeared in stories filled with plant imagery. (*Adventure* no. 428, 1973.)

ancient Egyptian costume with, for some reason, go-go style high-heeled boots, the goddess-superheroine was accompanied by a talking myna bird named Tut. The mod goddess had brains as well as beauty—she was, after all, a high school teacher. She accomplished her magic by making up poetry on the spot (To put out a fire, she says, "Oh blaze that burns and flames and flashes,/reduce yourself to cooling ashes!") and by doing solid research. At the conclusion of issue no. 1, she reveals that she knew how to banish an ancient Egyptian villain called Scarab by looking up the method in books about magic. "Proving," says the school principal, "that knowledge is the most *valuable* thing!" Isis was a good role model for young girls, and she lasted until 1978.

The New Teen Titans, a revamping of the old *Teen Titans,* began in 1980. Written by Marv Wolfman and drawn by George Pérez, it was DC's answer to Marvel's "X" comics. Wonder Girl, still wearing the costume that had been designed for her in 1969, was finally given some super-powered girlfriends: the darkly mystic Raven,

daughter of a demon and a human woman, and Starfire, a zaftig, golden-skinned alien princess with big hair. Starfire seemed to be DC's answer to Storm, and the character's leading role in the group was closely similar to that of Storm in the X-Men. Also like Storm, her eyes were drawn without irises or pupils. Eventually, exotic characters without irises or pupils in their eyes became a regular feature in comic books. Such insignificant problems as exactly how they could see were grandly ignored.

The book was filled with romance between the girl and boy team members, and between new super-powered teenagers who came and went from story to story. Starfire and Robin were sweet on each other. Lilith, a character from the original *Teen Titans,* was in love with a beautiful winged alien named Azrael. In a 1984 story, he flies above New York City with her in his arms. They kiss in mid-air as he says, "I love you, Lilith." But sometimes the romances between the superteens ended tragically, as when Lilith discovered that she was really a goddess and that

149. The success of Marvel's *X* titles led DC to revamp their teenage superhero group, the Teen Titans, and add more superheroines to the cast. In this *New Teen Titans* panel, Wonder Girl, carried over from the old *Teen Titans*, discusses love with Starfire, a zaftig alien princess with big hair and no pupils. (*New Teen Titans* no. 29, 1983.)

150. To appeal to young female readers, the *New Teen Titans* included romantic involvements between the super-powered characters. A romantic moment turns scary as Azrael, a winged alien, carries Teen Titan Lilith over New York's Washington Square Park. Story by Marv Wolfman, art by José Luis García López and Romeo Tanghal. (*New Teen Titans* no. 7, 1984.)

Equal Opportunity Employer

Three Women and a Duck...
and a host of assorted goblins, things, heroes, and hulks make up the expanding Marvel cast of characters. Absolutely no creature is denied admission to the Marvel family because of sex, color, creed, or cosmic background. Each has an equal opportunity to become a star. And each is one more reason we've been able to grow into **Marvel Entertainment Group**, comic magazines plus a whole lot more! Think of Marvel Entertainment and our cast of thousands for your next TV, motion picture or another production. Just use your imagination.

Contact
MARVEL ENTERTAINMENT GROUP
Alice Donenfeld
Vice President Business Affairs
575 Madison Avenue
New York, N.Y. 10022

151. A 1980 advertisement from the weekly entertainment trade newspaper, *Variety.* Sixteen years later, with anti-affirmative action feelings sweeping a more conservative nation, it is doubtful whether Marvel Comics would use the term "Equal Opportunity Employer" in an ad. Besides which, by 1996, the comic books starring all of the above women characters (and the duck) had long been canceled.

152. The Hulk was Dr. Bruce Banner, a scientist who regularly turned into a giant green monster after accidental exposure to a gamma-ray bomb. His cousin, attorney Jennifer Walters, became the Savage She-Hulk after an emergency transfusion with his blood. Stan Lee himself created this female version of the Hulk and wrote the script for her origin story, which was penciled by John Buscema and inked by Chic Stone. (*The Savage She-Hulk* no. 1, February 1980.)

she must stay on Olympus with the Greek gods. In a two-handkerchief scene, the lovers part. "From the time I saw the gold and marble temples of Zeus," Lilith sadly tells her winged boyfriend, ". . . I knew here was where my *destiny* lay. Although my heart *aches* to part with you, I have *no choice*." The sobbing Azrael, who strongly resembles a Greek god himself, repeats, "I love you, Lilith . . . and I . . . I can *never* forget you . . ." Not surprisingly, *The New Teen Titans* was another girl favorite.

Back at Marvel, the superheroine books kept coming, but by the eighties, with Stan Lee's editorial influence waning—he was by now Marvel's publisher, instead of editor—and with the original feminist influence weakened or forgotten, they were getting sillier.

Just as Jessica Drew had been inoculated by irradiated spider's blood, in 1980 the Hulk's cousin, Jennifer Walters, received a transfusion of the big green guy's gamma-radiated blood, and became the Savage She-Hulk. She grew big and green, and in the process busted out of most of her clothes. She also acquired a bad temper, but stayed smarter than her cousin, whose entire vocabulary was often limited to such exclamations as "Hulk smash!" *The Official Handbook of*

the Marvel Universe lists She-Hulk's vital statistics as "Height: 6'7", Weight: 650 lbs."

In 1981, new editor Jim Shooter came up with yet another superheroine: the Dazzler. In what had by now become a tradition, disco singer Alison Blaire was a mutant. Her powers, however, were less than impressive. While the other mutants flew, she got around on roller skates, and her one special ability was to create a kind of cosmic light show when she performed. She used her psychedelic colored lights to blind and dazzle bad guys who threatened her. Because of her comparatively weak powers, the Dazzler's adventures often harkened back to Marvel's earlier romances or teen comics. Talent contests were a common theme in the earlier teen comics and, in the Dazzler's first issue, she won a talent contest against the Enchantress, that same troublemaker who had tried to destroy the Avengers in 1970. The year 1982 found her romantically involved with one of the X-Men. The Angel, aka Warren Worthington, was a rich, handsome blond guy who just happened to have wings sprouting from his shoulder blades, like Azrael from *The Teen Titans.* But the character of the Angel had been created first. In a scene that predates the one from *The New Teen Titans,* Angel takes Dazzler for

153. The alter egos of superheroines are usually either scientists or pursue traditional women's professions such as teaching. Although the Savage She-Hulk loses most of her clothes when she goes into action, her alter ego defies genre conventions by being a criminal defense lawyer. David Anthony Kraft wrote this story, and the art was by Mike Vosburg and Chic Stone. (*The Savage She-Hulk* no. 2, March 1980.)

154. Perhaps the oddest superheroine of the 1980s was the Dazzler, created by Jim Shooter when he succeeded Stan Lee as Marvel's editor-in-chief. Alison Blaire is a disco diva who becomes a roller-skating crime fighter whose one mutant power is to blind and confuse her opponents with spectacular, psychedelic lights. This panel shows her fighting the Enchantress, and was drawn by John Romita, Jr. and Alfredo Alcala. (*The Dazzler* no. 1, March 1981.)

155. The Dazzler's super power was inspired by disco, but the depictions of her use of it seem more drawn from the psychedelic sixties than the nightclubbing seventies. (*The Dazzler* no. 1, March 1981.)

a spin above moonlit Manhattan. The caption describes her as "feeling the gentle strength of Warren Worthington's arms . . . she is filled with a deepening sense of awe . . ." High above the World Trade Center they share a romantic kiss, and the caption tells us, "She is drunk with the magic of the moment . . . and with the *tenderness* of the man in whose arms she is entangled."

Disco was already dead, but the Dazzler continued for forty-two issues.

The eighties, inspired by a new Republican administration, was a leaner and meaner time than previous decades. In keeping with the mood of the times, the first major new superheroine to emerge from these years was an assassin. Created by artist Frank Miller, Elektra made her first appearance in *Daredevil,* the comic book series he was writing and drawing. Elektra Natchios, daughter of the Greek ambassador, had been the college sweetheart of Daredevil's alter ego, Matt Murdock. Embittered by her father's assassination, she became an expert at martial arts, and an assassin and bounty hunter. In Miller's 1982 story, the paths of the two former lovers cross, and they find themselves on opposing sides of the law. In a dramatic and moving climax, Elektra is herself assassinated by a hired killer named Bullseye, and she dies in Daredevil's arms. This might have been the end of the lovely and deadly ninja, but Elektra was too good a character to give up, so in 1984 Marvel released the four-part *Elektra Saga,* consisting of the original Elektra story from the earlier

Daredevil, with extra pages added. Then, in 1986, the tragic heroine starred in her own eight-issue limited series, written by Miller and drawn by Bill Sienkiewicz. The series is well written and beautifully drawn in Sienkiewicz's experimental style, which is characterized by extensive use of collage techniques. It is also, however, graphically violent to an extreme that had never before seen on the pages of a comic book. There are some scenes in which characters literally look like fugitives from a butcher's freezer. It ends on a curious right-wing note, effectively approving the threat of nuclear war as a way to intimidate adversaries, a philosophy also espoused by the then-president of the United States, Ronald Reagan.

It was not made clear just when Elektra's 1986 adventure took place—was this a prequel? Obviously, the story must have happened before Miller's 1982 comic, because after that, Elektra was dead.

Or was she? In the last book of the four-part *Elektra Saga,* ninja warriors have stolen her body and brought it to an abandoned church where

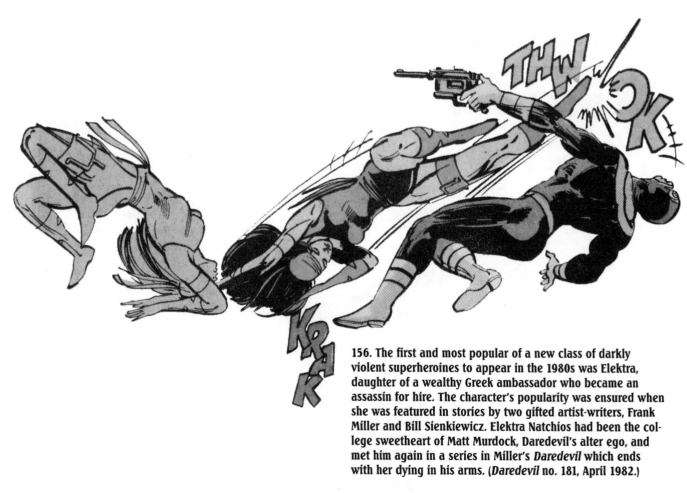

156. The first and most popular of a new class of darkly violent superheroines to appear in the 1980s was Elektra, daughter of a wealthy Greek ambassador who became an assassin for hire. The character's popularity was ensured when she was featured in stories by two gifted artist-writers, Frank Miller and Bill Sienkiewicz. Elektra Natchios had been the college sweetheart of Matt Murdock, Daredevil's alter ego, and met him again in a series in Miller's *Daredevil* which ends with her dying in his arms. (*Daredevil* no. 181, April 1982.)

157. Like many other comic characters, Elektra's death was less final than it appeared. Elektra was a gymnast, trained in the martial arts by a secret Asian organization called the Hand, and a group of ninja warriors claimed her body and brought her back to life to star in Bill Sienkeiwicz's series *Assassin* (1986, top), and Miller's *Elektra Lives Again* (1990, right).

they attempt to resurrect her. During a battle between Daredevil and the ninja, her body disappears. Finally we see her climbing a mountain in the snow. The caption tells us: "He must never know. He must seek his own destiny, live the life he knows—and perhaps, in time, forget her." But as long as a vast comic-buying audience wanted to read more about Elektra, Daredevil was not going to forget her.

Comic book characters have a pesky habit of not staying dead. Phoenix, whose tragic death in 1980 sold so many copies of *X-Men*, turned out

158. The Elektra, Assassin stories, starring a dark and embittered Greek heroine, carried emotional weight because of the leaner and meaner times under America's new Republican administration. (*Daredevil* no. 181, April 1982.)

not really to have been Jean Grey at all, but a cosmic force that duplicated her body while the real Marvel Girl lay in suspended animation at the bottom of Jamaica Bay. And in 1990, Marvel Comics published Frank Miller's graphic novel, *Elektra Lives Again,* in which Daredevil, haunted by what may or may not be dreams of his dead love, begins to suspect that she is not, after all, really dead. In another beautifully drawn story (one that is almost as bloody as *Elektra, Assassin)* Elektra is of course still alive and has been hiding out in that old church, disguised as a nun. Using

some perversion of Christian ceremony, the mystic ninjas from the *Elektra Saga* bring her original assassin back to life. In the end, Elektra and her assassin kill each other and she dies once more in Daredevil's arms.

Mother of God, could this finally be the end of Elektra? No way. Marvel Comics brought her back again in 1995, this time with writing by D. G. Chichester and art by Scott MacDaniel and Hector Collazo.

Elektra was the only villainess besides Catwoman to become a heroine and star in her own comic book. But Catwoman, even when she was a villainess, never killed. Superheroines and superheroes had never killed before, but comics were changing with the times.

1985 saw the debut of another Marvel Comics heroine whose "get tough on crime" stance matched the mood of the eighties. She was Dagger, the female half of a supervigilante team, Cloak and Dagger. The young superwoman and -man had been runaways who, along with other homeless teenagers, were kidnapped by the mob and forced to serve as unwilling guinea pigs for a new drug, which killed all but the beautiful blonde Tandy Bowen and her troubled African American friend, Tyrone Johnson. These two somehow acquired superpowers from the drug—Tandy's powers of light and Tyrone's of darkness—and they spend their time attempting to destroy what they consider the forces of evil.

Cloak's and Dagger's ideas regarding evil that must be destroyed do not always seem to coincide with what is illegal in real life. The first issue of *Cloak and Dagger* starts with the two invading an adult bookstore, the kind with booths in the back where a customer can pay to talk to a "live nude girl," separated from each other only by a pane of glass. Objectionable as these places might be, they are not illegal. Furthermore, the young woman behind the glass is not even depicted as nude; she's wearing a low-cut evening gown. Paying fifty cents to talk to a "live girl in an evening gown" can hardly even be considered objectionable!

The point is made that the young women employed in this place are underage, but it is never proved in the comic that the owners know this. Dagger also admits that the girls probably weren't kidnapped. "There are other ways to force . . . runaways to do your will," she says. "Some you hold with promises of money . . . and some with shelter and food!" Again, this is hardly illegal, but Cloak enfolds the proprietor of the place in his cloak, sending him into a mysterious

159. The stories featuring Marvel's superhero team of Cloak and Dagger echoed the "get tough on crime" mood of the eighties. Dagger was drawn to look as ethereal and delicate as a ballet dancer and the two were depicted as friends, but their targets sometimes seemed to be condemned for lifestyle rather than law-breaking. (*Cloak and Dagger* no. 2, November 1983.)

160. Cloak and Dagger were two teenage runaways who were forced by the mob to try a new psychoactive drug. All the other teens who were given the drug died, but Tyrone Johnson (Cloak) and Tandy Brown (Dagger) gained the super powers that led to their careers as vigilantes. (*Cloak and Dagger* no. 4, January 1984.)

161. Cloak's super power enabled him to hurl evildoers into a mind-shattering darkness, while Dagger is shown here exercising her power of hurling living daggers of light. Art by Rick Leonardi and Terry Austin. (*Cloak and Dagger*, reproduced from original art.)

and unpleasant dark dimension from which he emerges on the brink of gibbering lunacy.

Dagger, although drawn by Rick Leonardi to look ethereal and delicate as a ballet dancer, is no nicer than Cloak. She possesses the power to hurl daggers of living light which shock the victims' nervous system, cause temporary paralysis, rob their life energy, and can cause death. In issue no. 2, she goes to see her fashion-model mother at a party in a Long Island mansion. Although the atmosphere doesn't really seem much more decadent than the average cocktail party, Dagger is disgusted enough to loose her light daggers on the partygoers. When the light show ends, the superpowered teenager stands amid a cluster of fallen bodies (including that of her mother) who look not merely dead, but really most sincerely dead. The accompanying copy never explains whether the unfortunate guests have been killed or simply immobilized, so it's reasonable to assume that an entire cocktail party has been slaughtered by Dagger for the crime of ultrasophistication.

162. The kids-in-space setups of television shows like *Space Family Robinson* and young adult science fiction novels like Robert A. Heinlein's *The Rolling Stones* came to comics in the 1980s in Marvel's *Power Pack*, with the added element that the four young heroes had super powers. Created and written by Louise Simonson, the characters were designed by June Brigman. They included sisters Katie and Julie Power and their two brothers. (*Power Pack Holiday Special* no. 1, 1992.)

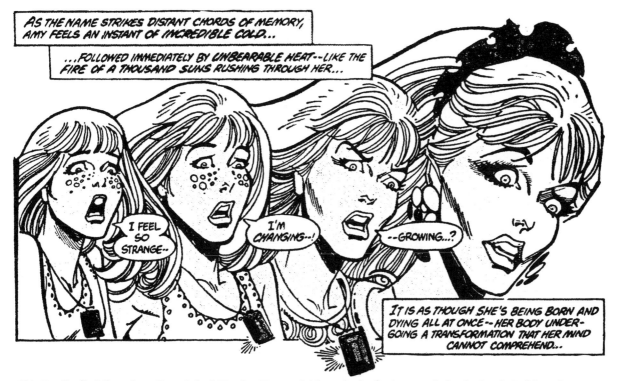

163. For the first time since the original *Wonder Woman*, DC launched a fantasy comic book aimed at girls and young women with a twelve-issue series, *Amethyst, Princess of Gemworld*, in 1983. Like Billy Batson, thirteen-year-old Amy Winston becomes an adult woman when she is transformed into Princess Amethyst. (*Amethyst, Princess of Gemworld* no. 1, May 1983.)

164. Amy not only becomes Princess Amethyst, but is transported to Gemworld, filled with fantasy characters including kings and queens, witches and ogres, and even a winged unicorn. Amethyst must use magical powers to battle various enemies, particularly the Dark Opal, and finds romance with the handsome Prince Topaz. (*Amethyst, Princess of Gemworld* no. 6, October 1983.)

165. In the 1980s, several comic book companies revived superheroines of the 1940s, including the independent Eclipse Comics, which brought back Valkyrie in stylish new stories written by Chuck Dixon. Art by Ernie Colón. (*Airboy* no. 46, January 1989.)

When they are not out wreaking havoc upon people whom they think deserve it, Cloak and Dagger take refuge at the Holy Ghost Church. Elektra, in her 1990 graphic novel, also hides out in an old church. A weird note of Christian metaphysics was seeping into superhero/heroine comics.

Also weird was Dagger's costume: a white jumpsuit with a navel-baring, dagger-shaped cutout at the chest. In real life the neckline would constantly be falling open, exposing more than even today's mainstream comics are allowed to reveal. We must assume that because the costume was magic, it stayed closed.

Weirdest of all, however, was the suggestion of racism in the depiction of the superpair. Why does the blonde woman become a force of light while an African American man is the force of darkness? Would it not have been more creative and original to make the African American character a force of light? Surely writer Bill Mantlo could not have realized the sort of stereotype he was abetting!

Not all the new superheroines who emerged in the eighties were so frightening. In 1984, two young super-powered sisters who were very different from Elektra and Dagger debuted, along with their super-powered brothers, in Marvel's *Power Pack*, created and written by Louise Simonson. June Brigman, who drew the earliest issues of the book, designed the characters of Katie Power (Energizer) and Julie Power (Lightspeed) along with their brothers Alex (Gee) and Jack (Mass Master). The Power siblings, an older brother and sister set and a younger brother and sister set were a sort of superpowered Bobbsey Twins. They had received their unique powers from Aelfyre Whitemane, an alien creature who resembled a friendly white

166. During World War II, Black Angel and Black Venus were joined by another comic book aviator named Valkyrie, who costarred with Airboy in the popular *Air Fighters* and *Airboy Comics*. Valkyrie was a German pilot who had led the deadly Air Maidens squadron, but after encountering Airboy, she realized the evils of Nazism and joined the Allied cause. The characteristic look of her and Airboy's adventures was set by Fred Kida. (*Air Fighters Comics* no. 7, 1944.)

167. In 1987, independent comic book company Eclipse revived Valkyrie in several series of new comics edited by cat yronwode. Valkyrie had been captured and placed in suspended animation by the skull-headed villain Misery inside his gigantic mold-encrusted plane, the Airtomb. After her revival, she joins up with the new Airboy, son of the original, and with Sylvia Lawton, the Black Angel, who has become U.S. ambassador to the Soviet Union. (*Valkyrie, Prisoner of the Past*, Eclipse Books, 1987.)

168. Also published by Eclipse was *Portia Prinz of the Glamazons,* a literate parody of Wonder Woman, six issues of comics drawn and written by Richard Howell. Portia Prinz of Glamazon Island was "the world's leading pseudo-intellectual super-heroine." (*Portia Prinz of the Glamazons* no. 1, December 1986.)

horse. The names that the kids took for themselves described their powers: Katie could store energy and fire it from her body, while Julie could fly with the speed of light. Alex had power over gravity, and Jack could take gaseous form and compress his mass to become tiny. Consistently well written and well drawn, *Power Pack* appealed to children as well as to adults who preferred more fanciful, less violent stories, and it lasted for seven years.

Although the Power sisters were different and refreshing, they were also part of a team. Dagger, too, was part of a team. Fewer and fewer superheroines starred in their own books as the

decade progressed. A rare exception was DC's Amethyst, Princess of Gemworld, one of the best and most charming superheroines to emerge from those years. Amethyst, the creation of Dan Mishkin and Gary Cohn and drawn in a decorative, fairy-tale style by Ernie Colón, was very much a fairy tale in the tradition of the original *Wonder Woman.* It told the story of thirteen-year-old Amy Winston who received, as a birthday present, an amethyst necklace which transported her to magical Gemworld, where she was a princess. Just as young Billy Batson turned into a grown man when he said the magic words to become Captain Marvel, adolescent Amy

169. Louise Grant, the Blonde Phantom of the 1940s, returned as a matronly sidekick for Jennifer Walters in John Byrne's series of She-Hulk comics. (*The Sensational She-Hulk* no. 40, June 1992.)

ANYBODY WHO WAS *DOPEY* ENOUGH TO THINK YOU COULD *REALLY* BE SKIPPING ROPE IN THE NUDE...

...*DESERVES* TO HAVE *WASTED* HIS MONEY ANYWAY!

NOW, *COME ON!* SPEAKING OF WASTE...

170. John Byrne's issues of the She-Hulk comic were widely noted for their good-natured satire, which often included joking references to Marvel staffers. In this example, Byrne removes the fourth wall and shows us editor Renee Witterstaetter talking with She-Hulk. (*The Sensational She-Hulk* no. 40, June 1992).

Winston was transformed into a beautiful young woman in Gemworld. Her new home was a wonderful place of kings and queens, witches and ogres, all with the powers and the names of jewels. The princess's enemies were Dark Opal, Sardonyx, and Carnelian, the Red Prince; her friends bore names such as Witch-mother Citrina, Lady Turquoise, and Princess Emerald. There was even a very handsome love interest, Prince Topaz, and to top off the fantasy, the princess was given a winged unicorn to ride.

Amethyst, Princess of Gemworld tapped into a familiar fantasy or myth that had been used before in comics: a child of royal or superhuman birth is spirited away from her real parents and adopted by others. It worked for Superman, and it worked for Amethyst. The first issue of the book, which started in 1983, began with this caption: "You have shared the child's dream: the dream of a *lost legacy*—that your parents are not

really your parents . . . that you are a *foundling,* a changeling child—and the orphaned heir to a *mystic throne!*" In issue no. 3, the evil Sardonyx explains further. He reminds Dark Opal of the time that the dark lord invaded Castle Amethyst. Lord and Lady Amethyst, he relates, knew that they would be slain, "but they sought to buy time for their infant heir to be saved—And soon, at Lady Amethyst's command, the witch-mother Citrina took the babe to another world . . . called *Earth!* There she was raised by *adopted* parents, with no knowledge of her *true identity.* . . ."

Amethyst began as a twelve-issue maxiseries, but reader response was so strong that it became a regular title, lasting sixteen more issues. As can be seen in the letters pages, at least some of that reader response was from women and girls. The gemstone princess shared enough of the winning characteristics of the Amazon princess to gain some of Wonder Woman's young female fans. A letter from eleven-year-old Joy Hunsberger reads, "I used to make *Wonder Woman* comics my only book, until I spied a comic book with Amethyst on the back of a flying unicorn."

In issue no. 6 of the series, Cathy Edwards starts her letter, "Amethyst is fabulous. She's smart, gutsy, has opponents worth fighting and a whole universe to discover." She continues with a piece of criticism: "Cover her up. The costume is fine if you give her an inch or two of material in the right places." Editor Karen Berger obligingly answers, "As you've already noticed in *Amethyst* no. 5, Cathy, our purple princess is sporting a short skirt. We thought she needed a more fantasy-looking costume, and I think the skirt does the trick." Not all future editors would be so sensitive to the comments of their female readers.

By the mid-eighties, Marvel and DC were no longer the only players on the comics field. Independently published comics, many boasting

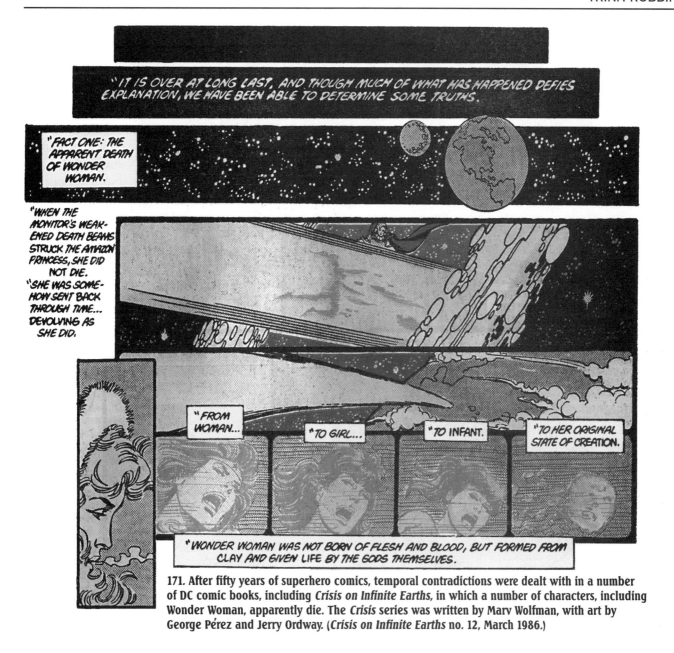

"IT IS OVER AT LONG LAST, AND THOUGH MUCH OF WHAT HAS HAPPENED DEFIES EXPLANATION, WE HAVE BEEN ABLE TO DETERMINE SOME TRUTHS.

"FACT ONE: THE APPARENT DEATH OF WONDER WOMAN.

"WHEN THE MONITOR'S WEAK-ENED DEATH BEAMS STRUCK THE AMAZON PRINCESS, SHE DID NOT DIE.
"SHE WAS SOME-HOW SENT BACK THROUGH TIME... DEVOLVING AS SHE DID.

"FROM WOMAN...

"TO GIRL...

"TO INFANT.

"TO HER ORIGINAL STATE OF CREATION.

"WONDER WOMAN WAS NOT BORN OF FLESH AND BLOOD, BUT FORMED FROM CLAY AND GIVEN LIFE BY THE GODS THEMSELVES.

171. After fifty years of superhero comics, temporal contradictions were dealt with in a number of DC comic books, including *Crisis on Infinite Earths,* in which a number of characters, including Wonder Woman, apparently die. The *Crisis* series was written by Marv Wolfman, with art by George Pérez and Jerry Ordway. (*Crisis on Infinite Earths* no. 12, March 1986.)

lushly printed full-color pages on heavy paper, had become serious contenders. Sadly, instead of attempting to break new ground with original concepts, most of them seemed to be Marvel/DC wannabees. Most superheroines introduced by these new companies were either not worth mentioning or were simply members of yet another superteam.

Eclipse Comics, however, under the editorship of cat yronwode, brought back two airborne heroines from the golden-age of comics: Black Angel and Valkyrie. Valkyrie (not to be confused with the ultrafeminist who stirred up trouble among the Avengers in 1970) had first appeared in the adventures of a World War II flying ace

named Daredevil (not to be confused with Elektra's boyfriend), drawn by artist Fred Kida in 1944. She had started as a German adversary to the hero, but his good looks and bravery had won her and the flying Air Maidens she led over to the Allied side. Thereafter, she had shared in many of Airboy's adventures as a strong sidekick.

In Eclipse's 1987 revival, a new Airboy, son of the original Airboy, rescued Valkyrie from her imprisonment by a golden-age villain named Misery. For almost forty years, she had lain in suspended animation in Misery's Airtomb, an ancient, mold-covered plane. After waiting forty years, Valkyrie finally starred in her own book.

Written by Chuck Dixon, with art by Paul Gulacy and Willie Blyberg, *Valkyrie, Prisoner of the Past* tells the story of the revived Valkyrie, now living in New York City, who is kidnapped by the Soviet Union and made to stand trial for a war crime she swears she didn't commit. She stands accused of the 1941 bombing—and annihilation—of Lubov, a Russian village that had been turned into a sanctuary for children. In vain, Valkyrie insists, "I *never* went on *terror bombing*

172. For several years after the relaunch of Wonder Woman in 1986, a number of women creators worked on the series, including writer Mindy Newell and artist Jill Thompson. This drawing by Ramona Fradon appeared in the 1989 *Wonder Woman Annual* which showcased the work of ten different women cartoonists. (*Wonder Woman Annual* no. 2, September 1989.)

missions. I only flew against *military* targets!" And, "I was flying for the allies at the time of the Lubov raid." Finally she asks her interrogator, a gruesome, metal-helmeted guy named Steelfox: "You are so *sure* I am guilty. Why *is* that?"

"I *am* sure, murderer . . ." he replies, ". . . as only an *eyewitness* can be. *I* was one of those children! I saw my sister of only *four* years burn to *death* in the flames!" He continues, "I *gained* this steel head-piece to replace the structure of my fractured skull. I was six years old." He screams with fury: "It *was* you! I *saw* you! I saw your *plane!*"

The United States ambassador to Russia just happens to be Sylvia Lawton, the original Black Angel, who had flown with Valkyrie back in the forties. Convinced of the aviatrix's innocence, Sylvia, now an old woman, becomes her defense attorney, aided by her young African American assistant, Holly. Sylvia finds a potential witness to testify on Valkyrie's behalf—an ex-Air Maiden named Anna Mahlmann—but she lives in East Germany (this takes place before the Berlin Wall went down). Holly, who has learned of Sylvia's secret wartime identity, dresses up in Sylvia's Black Angel costume—a *real* Black Angel—and gets the old woman out of Berlin.

Sylvia, Holly, and Anna Mahlmann show up at Valkyrie's trial in the nick of time. Anna shocks everyone by testifying that Valkyrie didn't bomb Lubov, because: "*I* led the raid against the village of Lubov." With tears streaming down her face, the old woman continues: ". . . shortly after Valkyrie went over to the Allied side." The Nazi commander informed the Air Maidens that they needed a new Valkyrie, she continues. "As I was closest in height and build to the original Valkyrie I was chosen to take her place. They dressed me in her clothes and made me wear a black wig. I agreed to this out of loyalty to my country."

But the false Valkyrie didn't know she was bombing children. "It wasn't until later that they revealed the truth to us," she testifies. "I never saw the children, I swear to you. The raid was too swift. But still I see their faces when I close my eyes."

In a very moving last sequence, while the exonerated Valkyrie flies home to America along with Holly, who clutches a package containing the Black Angel costume, Anna Mahlman hangs herself in her prison cell. Death comes for the old woman and, as she follows his spectral form into the afterlife, she becomes once again a young and beautiful Air Maiden.

In 1986, Eclipse published Richard Howell's *Portia Prinz of the Glamazons,* subtitled "World's leading pseudo-intellectual superheroine." The six-issue miniseries parodied Wonder Woman, and related the adventures of Princess Portia and her friends on Glamazon Island. The glamazons all have mystic powers, but what Portia does more than anything else is read lots of books, and talk even more about all the books that she's read. It was a lighthearted spoof; and Portia Prinz was a kind of highly literate Diana Prince.

173. The new, new "old" Wonder Woman. Between the "death" of Wonder Woman in the *Crisis* series and her relaunch in a new series of monthly comic books, Trina Robbins collaborated with writer Kurt Busiek in a last tribute to the original Marston-Peter character in a four-issue series that revived Atomia, one of the most memorable villains of the original comics. (*Wonder Woman*, 1986.)

Another golden-age superheroine was revived when John Byrne took over *She-Hulk* in 1989: the Blonde Phantom. Having put on some years and not a few pounds, Louise Grant became a kind of sidekick to the big green superheroine and shared in many of her adventures. To differentiate the book from *The Savage She-Hulk*, which had lasted two years, Byrne's version was called *The Sensational She-Hulk.* Byrne wrote and drew the adventures of the character he nicknamed Shulkie, and played it for good-natured satire. He also removed the fourth wall, that barrier between fictional characters and their readers. She-Hulk often addressed the audience, and seemed to know that she was in a comic book. The cover of issue no. 39 finds her draped in the arms of a hairy dude named Mahkizmo. Regular readers knew that their She-Hulk would never take so helpless a pose; neither would she go for this guy, who is a satire on sexism. So the superheroine explains to them on the cover:

"Don't get the wrong idea . . . I'm only doing this because it makes a good cover!!" Making her first appearance in the book on page 4, the green superheroine comments, "Well! It's about *time!* I was beginning to think you'd *forgotten* whose *book* this is!"

Over at DC, they were having problems with the continuity of their supercharacters. Most of their major characters, like Superman, Batman, and Wonder Woman, had been running without interruption for almost fifty years. Readers who were willing to accept that a super-powered baby from another planet could be adopted by Earth parents and grow up to fight injustice in tights and cape nonetheless insisted on a certain amount of realism: why wasn't anybody aging? DC's answer, for a while, was to create two Earths—Earth One and Earth Two. The original golden-age superheroes and -heroines, now aged, lived on Earth Two, while their younger counterparts lived on Earth One. But soon even the two

174. A panel from the *Wonder Woman* anthology featuring the work of twelve women artists and writers. (*Wonder Woman Annual* no 2, September 1989.

Earths grew unwieldy. Eventually there was only one alternative: kill 'em all off and start all over again. In *Crisis on Infinite Earths,* a yearlong maxiseries, every DC character participated in a battle with evil extraterrestrial forces. A goodly number of them were killed off, including Supergirl, Wonder Woman, and everybody on Earth Two.

By now we know that no one stays dead in comics. The idea of killing the characters off was to then reinvent them. While George Peréz was reworking the amazing Amazon, I filled in with a four-part limited series that was a last tribute to the original Marston-Peter *Wonder Woman.* Collaborating with writer Kurt Busiek, I brought back Diana's old adversary, Atomia, queen of the atom world.

A new *Wonder Woman* no. 1, written and drawn by George Peréz and retelling Princess Diana's origin from a different perspective, appeared in 1987. Peréz drew the book for twenty-four issues, and continued to write it for thirty-eight more issues. Another dimension to *Wonder Woman* was added when Mindy Newell took over the writing in 1988 and introduced themes of special interest to women, such as menstruation and teen suicide. In 1989, DC produced a special *Wonder Woman* annual, which included art by ten different women cartoonists, after which the book was taken over by Jill Thompson for the next two years. After almost fifty years, women were finally drawing *Wonder Woman.*

11

*C*hick books
don't sell!

–generic man
representing the
comic book
industry speaking to
Li'l Silvie. *Silver Sable
and the Wild Pack*
no. 35 (1995)

In 1940, a minor superhero named Doctor Fate debuted in *More Fun Comics* no. 55, and ran until issue no. 98. Doctor Fate was Kent Nelson, who donned the helmet of a supernatural being named Nabu the Wise and gained mystic powers. In 1987, the golden-age superhero was revived by DC Comics. Young Eric Strauss, the new Doctor Fate, had to merge with his stepmother, Linda, in order to become the golden-helmeted superhero. Thus, Doctor Fate now possessed both sexes. Then, Eric died in battle and Linda temporarily became Doctor Fate all by herself. Now Doctor Fate was all-female. To complicate things further, Linda died, too, and both Eric's and Linda's souls were reborn in other bodies. Writer J. M. DeMatteis added more than a touch of East Indian mysticism to the story; there was much dying, being reborn, playing of musical souls, and mystic

175. Doctor Fate casts a spell. Story by William Messner-Loebs, art by Scot Eaton, Peter Gross and Romeo Tanghal. (*Doctor Fate* no. 32, 1992.)

switching of sexes in the series until finally William Messner-Loebs took it over in 1991, and turned Doctor Fate permanently into a woman.

She was Inza Nelson, wife of Kent Nelson, the original Doctor Fate, and she reacted to her new power differently than her husband or, in fact, any other superhero had ever reacted to having superpowers. She made things nicer. In issue no. 28, a really nasty gang member grabs a woman's purse. When Inza/Doctor Fate intervenes, he sputters, "I'll *kill* you, man! *Kill* you! My men'll *find* you and *rip you up!* . . . No chick messes with *me!* I'll do the job on you *myself!* Make it *hurt!* Then I'll . . ." The guy is beyond redemption, or is he? Doctor Fate gestures mystically, and a little golden globe decorated with an Egyptian ankh appears. Thick black smoke starts to pour from the thug's eyes, nose, mouth, and ears. She has burned the badness out of him! Suddenly he is smiling, transformed. He returns the purse to the woman, saying, "Here. Sorry I took this. It was cruel and meanspirited of me."

After this incident, a man on the street comments, touching a nearby brick wall, "Funny thing is, these bricks used to be dirtier, cracked. They look *newer* since Dr. Fate started visiting."

An old woman chimes in, "Somethin' else . . . the street used to be *uneven* . . . the sidewalk was cracked. Now everything on this street's smooth as glass. And the smooth area goes a little further every day . . ."

The new female Doctor Fate is cleaning up her neighborhood! Her husband Kent, the original Doctor Fate, notices the difference in their thinking. In issue no. 35, walking through the Fate-improved neighborhood, he muses, "In all the time I was *Doctor Fate,* it never *once* occurred to me to use the power this way. All I did was get into *fight* after *fight.* I never tried to build *anything.*" In the next issue, Kent briefly becomes Doctor Fate again to battle a gigantic green, fanged monster. While fighting with the slavering brute, he thinks, "How would *Inza* handle this? She'd find *some* constructive angle. Probably give him a *job.* No struggle, no violence, everybody happy." The differences between the male and female Doctor Fates are similar to the differences between the original Wonder Woman, as created by William Moulton Marston, and most of the superpowered men in comics. Princess Diana also

176. The Jaguar's secret identity was María de Guzmán, a Brazilian college student going to school in the United States. Story by William Messner-Loebs, art by Rod Wigham and Pam Eklund. (*The Jaguar* no. 10, June 1992.)

always used her powers constructively, and only fought defensively.

Obviously, writing good women characters is not something that only women can do, and throughout the history of comic books there have been certain male writers besides Marston whose names pop up again and again in connection with outstanding superheroines. Otto Binder was one of these, as is Chris Claremont. William Messner-Loebs is another.

At the same time that he was writing *Doctor Fate*, Messner-Loebs was also scripting *The Jaguar* for DC comics, another in a long line of cat-based superheroines. Actually, the Jaguar was another

character who had started out as a man, in Archie Comics from the sixties, but Messner-Loebs turned him into a her: Brazilian college student María De Guzmán. The teaming of the naive young woman, new to this country, with her rich-bitch roommate, blonde cheerleader Tracy Dickerson, produced a superheroine version of the earlier teen girl comics.

Messner-Loebs' stories always maintain an element of humor. In issue no. 10, Tracy has found out that Maria is really the Jaguar. Jealously trying to one-up her roommate, Tracy gets her own Jaguar costume and pretends to be the superheroine. But in a battle with a real

177. Black Orchid and her roommate set out on their journey. Story by Dick Foreman, art by Jill Thompson. (*Black Orchid* no. 2, October 1993.)

178. Black Orchid and one of her sisters in the Amazon rain forest. Written by Neil Gaiman, art by Dave McKean. (*Black Orchid*, DC Comics Inc., 1991.)

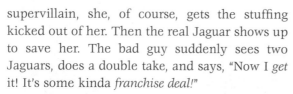

179. Rogue, a member of the X-Men, starred in a four-issue miniseries in 1995. Story and art by Howard Mackie, Mike Wieringo and Terry Austin. (*Rogue* no. 4, April 1995.

supervillain, she, of course, gets the stuffing kicked out of her. Then the real Jaguar shows up to save her. The bad guy suddenly sees two Jaguars, does a double take, and says, "Now I *get* it! It's some kinda *franchise deal!*"

After the Jaguar has beaten the bad guy, she visits banged-up Tracy in her hospital bed and, ever the Pollyanna, enthuses, "I am *glad* the doctor said you only have a small concussion and cracked ribs!" She adds, "I am *glad* you discovered my secret. . . . Now we can be *partners*. . . ! And fight *evil* together for ever and ever!"

Poor Tracy, with her head in a bandage, huge Band-Aids on her face, clutches her teddy bear and looks less than enthusiastic about the prospect. She thinks, "Oh, God. How do I get out of *this*?"

Messner-Loebs left *Doctor Fate* and *The Jaguar* to take over *Wonder Woman*. He imbued the Amazon princess with the same lack of cynicism he had given to the Jaguar. After all, both were earnest immigrants from another culture, new to many of America's ways. When Wonder Woman returns from an epic adventure in outer space, during which she and a Russian female astronaut were kidnapped and enslaved by a woman-hating alien race, she finds that her native island, Themiscyra, has disappeared, and she is forced to take a job waiting tables at a taco joint. But Messner-Loebs' Wonder Woman takes her waitress job as seriously as she had taken fighting bad guys. When her supervisor yells because she took time away from Taco Whiz for crime fighting, the Amazon solemnly agrees with her, volunteers to make it up by working overtime, and insists on a pay cut!

Doctor Fate, the Jaguar and, of course, Wonder Woman all were earlier characters redone for the nineties. Black Canary and Zatanna, other early DC superheroines, were also revived during the nineties. Actually, for almost twenty years, very few new superheroines had emerged in the pages of DC comics.

The elusive 1973 character, Black Orchid, also was reworked in 1989, when DC published a three-part miniseries by writer Neil Gaiman and artist Dave McKean. The story, which was later reprinted as a graphic novel, begins with an unusual twist—the book's heroine, Black Orchid, is killed on page ten. However, we soon learn that the murdered superheroine is but one of a number of plant clones which botanist Phil Sylvian created, using the DNA of his dead love, Susan. As the first Black Orchid dies, her consciousness enters the flower body of one of her sister clones. Why these flower women are invulnerable to bullets and can fly is never answered.

Before the new Black Orchid can find out much about herself, Doctor Sylvian is killed and all the other orchid clones are destroyed save a young flower child called Suzy. Black Orchid goes off with her little sister, on a search for identity which leads her to encounters with other DC characters: the mad villainess Poison Ivy,

180. Li'l Silvie, a strip drawn especially for the last issue of *Silver Sable*, to express the feelings of the writer, Gregory Wright. The man telling Silver Sable that "chick books don't sell" represents the comics industry. (*Silver Sable and the Wild Pack* no. 35, April 1995.)

Batman, and the plant-creature, Swamp Thing. By the end of her quest, she has found a sacred valley deep in the Amazon rain forest, and there she has planted seeds which will grow into sister Black Orchids.

By 1993, the lavender flowerwoman had become a dreamlike series, written by Dick Foreman and drawn first by Jill Thompson, then by Rebecca Guay. Thompson's and Guay's Black Orchid was more stylized and ethereal than McKean's moody photographic renditions. The new series began as an almost *Thelma and Louise*-type adventure, with Black Orchid and her roommate Sherilyn on the lam from an organization known as Logos. Logos is up to no good; their intention is to capture the Orchid and, as one of their officials says, get her "sliced, diced and analyzed."

181. Li'l Silvie, leading the other canceled Marvel superheroines, fights back. Drawn by Steven Butler and Pam Eklund. (*Silver Sable and the Wild Pack* no. 35, April 1995.)

182a. From
this . . .

182b. to this . . . in fifty years. Left, Harry G. Peter's Wonder Woman from the 1940s; right, Mike Deodato's version of the Amazon princess from the 1990s. (Right: *Wonder Woman* no. 92, December 1994.)

BUT BEHIND THE PANTHER APPEARS AN EVEN MORE SINISTER FORM!

CATWOMAN! SAVE ME FROM THAT PANTHER!

I WILL-- BUT ONLY IF YOU GIVE ME THAT CASE OF DIAMONDS YOU WERE HIRED TO DELIVER TO THE GOTHAM JEWELERS COMPANY!

183a. From this . . .

183b. to this . . . in fifty years. Left, the original version of Catwoman in a stylish 1940s dress; right, Jim Balent's Catwoman, one of the few DC superheroines with her own book in the 1990s.

184. Zatanna, a magician who wore a top hat, tails, and fishnet stockings, appeared in anthology books like *Adventure* and *World's Finest* in the 1960s and 1970s. Her first appearance was in *Hawkman* in a story by Gardner Fox, illustrated by Murphy Anderson. (*Hawkman* no. 4, 1964.)

As they flee the bad guys, Sherilyn and Black Orchid encounter fairies, dryads, a spore-creature from another planet, a Native American demon and, once more, the Swamp Thing. The women's buddy adventure comes to a sad and abrupt end in *Black Orchid* no. 7, when Sherilyn is killed by agents from Logos. After that, the flower woman's stories gradually grow dark, twisted, and more confusing. She becomes a goddess to an Amazonian tribe and little sister Suzy, who had been left behind in a fairylandlike other dimension, is brought back. Celtic and Pre-Columbian mythologies are mixed together helter-skelter, the flower woman gets meaner, and sister Suzy turns out to be a sensible little flower child and the more likable of the two characters. By the time the promising series self-destructed with issue no. 23, the once gentle Black Orchid had gone mad and was wreaking destruction on New York City.

Since the resurrection of the superhero in the 1960s, comics had been slowly growing darker and grimmer, and were being aimed at a more

185. Zatanna in 1993. Not sexy? Story by Lee Marrs, art by Esteban Maroto. (*Zatanna* no. 3, 1993.)

186. Black Canary brings her boots in to be fixed (top), and the shoe repair shop blows up (center). Next issue, she's back in high heels (bottom). Stories by Sarah E. Byam, art by Trevor Von Eeeden and Bob Smith. (Top and center, *Black Canary* no. 4, April 1993; bottom, *Black Canary* no. 5, May 1993.)

WE CAN'T STAY IN HERE, LADIES, THE WHOLE PLACE IS ON FIRE!!

187. Too butch? Black Canary sans wig, heels, and fishnets. Story by Sarah E. Byam, art by Leo Duranoña. (*Black Canary* no. 12, December 1993.)

and more solidly male audience. While a majority of supermen still starred in their own books, the superwomen were being relegated more and more to teams. In early 1995, Marvel comics published a four-issue miniseries starring one of their best superteam characters, Rogue, of the X-Men. Later that year they canceled their last superheroine book, *Silver Sable.*

By the nineties, comic books had become not merely a boy's club, but a Playboy Club. Using a kind of circular logic, editors at the major comic companies continue to produce sex object–heroines which appeal to a male audience. Their excuse for not adding strong female characters who might appeal to women is that "women don't read comics." Of course, as long as female comic characters are insulting to the average woman, she won't read comics.

When Mike Deodato took over as artist on *Wonder Woman* in 1994, and drew her as a barely-clothed hypersexual pinup, the magazine's circulation shot up. The same thing happened in 1993, when a revived Catwoman came out, drawn with enormous, exaggerated breasts by Jim Balent.

Catwoman's new look caused a controversy in the letters pages of the *Comics Buyer's Guide,* a weekly tabloid devoted to the comics industry. Editor Don Thompson wrote: "Recently we ran a letter from a woman complaining that Catwoman has become vastly more pneumatic for this series, with enormous breasts that would hamper her athletic prowess. The letters we have received in response are of two types: women agree and males disagree, with the males usually making the spurious claim that comic-book men are also drawn as excessively perfect physical specimens. This ignores the fact that the man's sexual characteristics are not stressed . . . and that men's athletic abilities are stressed far above and beyond their attractiveness.

"There is a message here for males, particularly those who bemoan the shortage of women comics fans, though those who most need to get it won't understand it."

Thompson neglected to comment on the fact that male comics readers seem to think that women must have enormous breasts in order to be "excessively perfect physical specimens," something that most women would definitely consider debatable. The 92 percent male comic book readership of the nineties expect, in fact demand that any new superheroines exist only as pinup material for their entertainment.

When writer Lee Marrs revived the magician Zatanna in 1993, Mike Gallaher, of Huntsville, Alabama, sent an indignant letter to the letters page: ". . . What Kim Yale [the editor] and Lee Marrs have delivered will fail, I think, to satisfy those looking for any nostalgic titillation. The Zatanna in these pages , although pretty, is certainly not sexy. . . . So what is supposed to be her appeal?" At the end of his letter, Gallaher repeats, "I don't think this will satisfy anyone—it's not sexy enough for the old time 'good girl' fans. . . ."

Gallaher doesn't seem to feel that a good story, well told and well drawn, can be sufficiently appealing for a superheroine comic. Artist Esteban Maroto draws Zatanna in an elegant and decorative style, which Gallaher is forced to admit is "pretty." So what, exactly, is his problem? The original Zatanna, from the sixties, wore fishnet hose and spike-heeled shoes. Marrs's and Maroto's Zatanna of the nineties has forsaken the fishnets for contemporary dress. Perhaps Gallaher wants the fishnets and spike heels back.

Another superheroine whose fishnets and high heels caused a controversy was Black Canary, revived in 1991 by Sarah Byam. In the letters page of issue no. 2, Valerie D. Macys of Phoenix, Maryland, wrote: ". . . How Dinah [Black Canary's alter ego] accomplishes all her dexterous moves in high heels has always baffled me. Try moving as Black Canary moves while wear-

188. "Bad girl" superheroines Glory and Avengelyne, drawn by Rob Liefeld, from Image Comics. (*Comics Scene* no. 53, Nov. 1995.)

ing heels. Ask any woman and she'll tell you it doesn't work. Most self-defense instructors tell women to ditch their heels if ever confronted by an attacker, especially if you need to run."

Editor Mike Gold, badly in need of sensitivity training, responds, "Hey, this is comics, folks—people can't really fly, if you get bitten by a radioactive spider you're likely to get sick and die, and if you put on a batcape and start fighting crime, you'll get tossed in the loony bin. In that context, fighting crime in high heels doesn't seem so weird . . ." Compare this answer to Gerry Conway's very sensitive editorial from *Ms. Marvel* in 1977. A lot had changed in less than twenty years.

Actually, writer Sarah Byam tried very hard to get her superheroine out of high heels and into a pair of sensible boots, but she didn't reckon with the (male) artist. In issue no. 4, Black Canary brings her boots, with a broken heel, into a shoe-repair shop to be fixed. The shop then blows up, presumably taking the boots along with it. For the rest of that issue, the superheroine goes barefoot. But in issue nos. 5, 6 and 7, artist Trevor Von Eeden has put her right back into the high-heeled boots!

When, by issue no. 9, Black Canary finally acquired a pair of low-heeled boots (and also ditched her rather impractical blonde wig), the comic book was flooded with angry letters from male readers: "I'm really going to miss the old costume! Now she looks so . . . butch!"—Kevin Knopp, Pittsburgh, Pennsylvania; "'Pain and Terror' is right! 'Pain', as in I (and my fellow male readers) mourning the passing of Canary's fishnets!"—Bob Kowalski, Detroit, Michigan; "I hate the new outfit! Canary looks butch—that's not her image."—Gregory Larson, Albany, New York; "This outfit is ugly, ugly, UGLY! Black Canary looks way too butch!!"—Larry Allison, Jr., New Cumberland, Wyoming.

In 1996, writer Chuck Dixon took another try at revamping the Black Canary, in an intelligently written one-shot titled *Birds of Prey.* He

189. Oracle and the newest Black Canary, from *Birds of Prey*, a one-shot written by Chuck Dixon, with art by Gary Frank. (*Birds of Prey* 1996.)

teamed her with Oracle, a wheelchair-bound heroine who had been Batgirl before she was crippled by the Joker. No longer able to fight crime as an athletic superheroine, Barbara Gordon, aka Oracle, has become a computer genius, and combats evil electronically. With Black Canary handling the physical part and Oracle supplying the scientific knowledge, they make a nice female brains-and-brawn team. Oddly enough, no one in comics had thought of pairing two costumed heroines before, but of

course it's a winning idea. Artist Gary Frank redesigned Black Canary nicely with styishly short, bleached-out hair and, finally, flat-heeled boots. Along with tossing out the wig, she has also dumped the fishnets, one hopes for good.

DC Comics has an online chat room called the DC Comics Online Forum. In response to the subject, Female Superheroes, this message was posted from "Jay Jay 29": "i would like to see MAXIMA to be bad. I do not know why, i would like to see her in a leather outfit where you can almost see her intire boobs and vjina [sic]."

Jay Jay 29 is probably very happy with the newest phenomenon in comic books, "bad girl" comics. Comics journalist Kurt Samuels describes bad girl comics in an article for the *Comics Buyers Guide's* Entertainment Edition: "These bad girls are not the same ones Donna Summer used to sing about in the disco era.

"Instead, today's comic bad girls are buxom characters who a) have had their families murdered by a psycho; or b) were abused as children and are now planning on controlling the world wearing only a string bikini while getting soaked by buckets of blood."

Samuels also writes that "the 'bad girl' comics . . . have been leading the way in sales." The combination of absurdly exaggerated sexual characteristics and blood may delight the Jay Jay 29s of the comics world, but the average woman finds them repellent and insulting. Also disturbing is the metaphysical mix that is added to so many bad girl comics; half-naked demons and angels abound in the pages of these books. One of the most popular, Lady Death, published by the aptly named Chaos! Comics, is a demoness who defeats Lucifer himself to become queen of Hell. The white-haired, white-eyed heroine, one more victim of the lack-of-pupil mania started by Storm of the X-Men, wears a skull at the crotch of her string bikini.

Angela, the heroine of a three-part miniseries from Image Comics, is an angel who would give Botticelli nightmares. She spends the entire three issues covered in blood, and little else. Writer Neil Gaiman is quite aware of the absurdity of a heaven populated by bare-bottomed, balloon-breasted figments of an adolescent boy's fantasy. When the popular superhero, Spawn, is

190. Lady Death, drawn by Steven Hughes. (*Lady Death Sneak Preview*, March 1995.)

brought to "Elysium . . . the home of angels," he comments, *"This is heaven? . . . It's beautiful. But why are they all—babes?"* Again, as he is escorted by other angels through the hallowed halls, he asks, *"Listen. Is there a reason why you all look like . . . uh . . . exotic dancers?"*

Of course, Spawn's questions are never answered, but Gaiman knows the reason. Jay Jay 29 wants it this way.

Neil Gaiman created another metaphysical heroine who is not a bad girl, although she might be a considered a bad grrrl—Death herself, in the *Sandman* series. *Sandman* is a product of DC Comics' Vertigo line, which publishes their more adult material, usually with a heavy emphasis on myth and/or metaphysics. Sandman himself is Dream, a member of the Endless, a gothic-looking family of seven sisters and brothers, all of whose names begin with D. His sister Death is portrayed as a perky teenager wearing heavy eye makeup and black jeans. The others are Destiny, Destruction, Desire, Despair, and Delirium. The youngest of Death's sisters, Delirium, is another engaging character. She speaks in prose poetry, using rainbow-colored speech balloons. But except for Dream, only Death has had her own comic book series, *Death, the High Cost of Living* (published as a three-part miniseries in 1993).

Gaiman based his story on the old belief that

191. Death herself. Story by Neil Gaiman, art by Chris Bachalo and Mark Buckingham. (*Death, The High Cost of Living*, 1993.)

192. Death talks about safe sex, from a four-page public service pamphlet, *Death Talks About Life.* Story by Neil Gaiman, drawn by Dave McKean. (1993.)

once in a century, Death comes down to Earth to spend a day in human form. In this case, she takes over the body of sixteen-year-old Didi, who has only one day to live before her weak heart gives out. Death spends her day with a teenage loner named Sexton Furnival. Sexton's terminal depression contrasts sharply with the newly human Death's cheerfulness. Everything is new and wonderful to her; she bites into an apple and comments, "Don't apples taste *great?* I mean the way they *taste*. And the *texture*. And the way when you chew them they kind of *crunch* and the juice runs out in your *mouth*."

Sexton doesn't understand. He replies, "They're just apples."

Later in the story, after tasting her first hot dog, Death asks, "Sexton, is the chemical after-taste the *reason* why people eat hot dogs? Or is it some kind of *bonus?*"

During Death's day on Earth, she and Sexton escape the clutches of a really disgusting evil wizard, and Death helps a 250-year-old witch find her missing heart. Sexton has gained a new outlook on life. Finally the day is over, and Death must die. In a very moving sequence, the now-dead Didi/Death raves about her day: "Oh,

193. Tank Girl was created by Jamie Hewlett and Alan Martin in England's comic magazine *Deadline;* their work was reprinted in the United States by Dark Horse Comics. (*Tank Girl,* 1995.)

194. Martha Washington faces the enemy, and their weapons blow up. Story by Frank Miller, art by Dave Gibbons. (*Happy Birthday, Martha Washington*, 1995.)

it was *wonderful*. It was filled with *people*. I got to breath and eat and . . . all *sorts* of stuff . . . and I heard a song and went in a taxi, and I had a hot dog and a bagel and. . . ."

Death tells her, "Take my hand, Didi," and the two girls merge into one. Had Death been portrayed as the usual skeletal Grim Reaper instead of a sweetly smiling girl with a smiley-

face button pinned to her lapel, this sequence would not have had the power to make grown women cry.

Because Death would rather not take anyone before their time, she also starred in a four-page public-service pamphlet entitled *Death Talks About Life* in which, using a banana, she demonstrated the use of a condom and talked about the

195. Ghost, who had been Elisa Cameron when alive, was created by Dark Horse Comics in 1995; art by H.M.Baker and Bernard Kolle. (From an SAF Studio promotional publication, 1995.)

reason for safe sex. The pamphlet, also written by Neil Gaiman, was dedicated to British comic publisher Don Melia, who died of AIDS in 1992.

Tank Girl is also a "bad grrrl," but whether she can be called a superheroine is debatable. Created in England by Jamie Hewlett and Alan Martin and originally published in the British comic magazine, *Deadline,* her stories have been reprinted in the United States by Dark Horse Comics. Tank Girl is a crusty little attitudinous Generation X-er with a mostly shaved head, a

bad cigarette and beer habit, and a mouth on her. The stories, though full of explosions and rude noises, are comparatively short on plot, but this much is clear: she lives in the Australian outback at some indiscernible future time, along with her half-human kangaroo boyfriend, Booga, her friends Jet Girl and Sub Girl, and a white-haired Aborigine named Steve. And she drives a tank.

Exactly what it is that Tank Girl does is harder to figure out. In the earliest stories she was some kind of government agent, but soon she became

196. Adastra, a goddesslike superheroine created by Barry Windsor-Smith. (*Young Gods,* 1996.)

197. Queenie (left) and Vector (right) in the fast-moving series *Heartbreakers,* written by Anina Bennett and drawn by Paul Guinan (*Heartbreakers* no. 1, 1996.)

an outlaw. Throughout her fragmented adventures, Tank Girl, though a roommate's nightmare, remains downright cute.

Unfortunately, *Tank Girl* was turned into a Hollywood movie, about which the less said the better. The film was adapted in graphic novel

198. Queenie, cloned from the late Professor Therese Sorensen, shows her prowess as a Beta bodyguard. (*Heartbreakers* no. 1, 1996.)

form by DC comics, which then published its own four-part version of *Tank Girl* with a different creative team under the Vertigo imprint. DC's Vertigo books are aimed at a college-aged audience. At their best they are, like the Sandman and Death stories, meaningful and intelligent. At their worst, they are pretentious and push the envelope of grossness to the tearing point. DC's *Tank Girl* was both. Writer Peter Milligan turned the story into a commentary on the *Odyssey* and James Joyce's *Ulysses,* just the thing for college students who have recently been introduced to both classics. In the grossness department, the reworked *Tank Girl* is probably no more disgusting than the original, but it lacks the wacky grrrl cuteness, which made the original Australian slacker so lovable.

It is also debatable whether Dark Horse's Martha Washington fits into

199. Gang member Beauty as Lady Justice. (*Lady Justice* no. 5, 1995.)

the superheroine category, but she is undeniably an outstanding female character. She first appeared in 1990, as the star of *Give Me Liberty,* a Dark Horse graphic novel written by Elektra creator Frank Miller and drawn by Dave Gibbons. Martha Washington is a young African American woman soldier, her short hair bleached out to pale blonde, living in a near-future American dystopia. Her well-crafted adventures stress the stupidity and futility of war. In one story, Martha finds herself in the middle of a civil war in the Louisiana swamps, fighting the "First Sex Confederacy," a militant feminist government. She and her enemy both wear complicated computerized armor, which goes haywire, and they escape their armor an instant before it self-destructs. Now they are simply two women—Martha facing a determined-looking Asian woman, each pointing huge souped-up assault weapons at the other. Both weapons blow up in their hands and, simultaneously, each reaches for her holstered handgun. The handguns don't

200. Publisher/creator Bill Black of AC Comics, in the Western outfit, shows the Femforce superheroines around, while artist Brad Gorby draws himself on the right, receiving some art criticism. (*Femforce,* 1996.)

201. Nightveil and Synn from the Femforce team; story by Bill Black, art by C. Bradford Gorby and Mark G. Heike (*Femforce* no. 95, 1996).

work! At this point, both women convulse with laughter and the last panel shows them sitting by a fire, swapping stories, and sharing rations.

There is no question about *Ghost,* also published by Dark Horse. She is indubitably a superheroine. Like her predecessor, Ghost Woman, from 1944, Ghost is already dead. Like Ghost Woman, Elisa Cameron can be seen only by malevolent supernatural creatures. The stories come from a number of different writers,

but the majority are contributed by Eric Luke. Scott Benefiel, George Dove, Adam Hughes, and Matt Haley are among the artists who draw her in an art nouveau–inspired style. Assuming that dead people can choose their own outfits, one has to wonder why Ghost chose to wear high-heeled boots and a very low-cut, white leather bustier.

Another superheroine from Dark Horse comes with an interesting history—in another

202. This page from Cutey Bunny explains the superrabbit's origin and her costume changes. (*Cutey Bunny,* 1985.)

203. Some panels from *Strange Attractors* showing superheroine comics within comics (*Strange Attractors*, 1994 and 1995.)

incarnation, she was Storm, leader of the X-Men. In 1984, Barry Windsor-Smith drew a special two-part *X-Men* story, written by Chris Claremont, titled "Lifedeath." Windsor-Smith also wrote and penciled a third part to the story, which was rejected by editor Bob Harras on the grounds that it condoned suicide. (In light of the fact that today's superheroes are often mass murderers, it does seem a bit odd to condemn a book because it condones suicide.) Over ten years later, Windsor-Smith reworked his rejected piece and changed the heroine into Adastra, a star of his 1996 Dark Horse comic, *Young Gods.* In the gracefully drawn story, which takes place in Africa, the goddesslike Adastra must deal with a famine and a tribal tradition that calls for one voluntary suicide for every birth. Windsor-Smith's story neither condones nor condemns suicide. Rather, it makes statements about ecology and about the eternal cycle of birth and death.

Vector and Queenie, from Dark Horse's 1996 series, *Heartbreakers,* are another brains-and-brawn team, but they are very different from Black Canary and Oracle. Vector and Queenie are clones of the now-dead Professor

204. A panel from *Action Girl*, written by Sarah Dyer and drawn by Elim Mak, in which Dyer voices her opinion of the outfits worn by contemporary superheroines (in this case, a superheroine named Neutrina). (*Action Girl*, no. 4.)

Therese Sorenson. Although they are both replicas of Sorenson, Vector, the Delta lab assistant and Queenie, the Beta bodyguard, have developed personalities of their own, wear their hair differently, and dress differently. The fast-moving story is written by Anina Bennett and drawn by her husband, Paul Guinan, an artist who—at last!—puts some meat on the bones of his female characters.

Possibly because they don't have to carry fifty or so years of superhero and -heroine baggage, independent comic publishers like Dark Horse have been a source of many of the more original and interesting recent superheroines. The prolific Neil Gaiman created but didn't write yet another superheroine for independent publisher Tekno Comics. Lady Justice is not one woman, but many different ones who, in turn, take on super powers when they don Justice's blindfold. The concept is good, but neither of the two writers has been able to explain why people rarely seem to notice that their heroines are wearing bandages over their eyes or how they can see while

205. Flying Girl talks to Action Girl about flying; art by Elizabeth Watasin. (*Action Girl Comics* no. 2, January 18, 1995.)

THE VERY FIRST APPEARANCE OF...

ACTION GIRL

CUT and COLOR
ACTIVITY PAGE

"The growing-out" hairstyle. Color various shades of purple.

where's a comb?!

Cheap headbands made from cut-up t-shirts. Color any color!!

On TV: Picket Fences or an old movie

ACTION GIRL STAYS HOME

get your crayons! get your scissors!

ACTION GIRL!!→

$10 "sports bra" — comfortable, supportive, and never comes undone. Color black.

Huge, comfy and optional (weather-depending) t-shirt. All cotton, well used but not washed enough. Color well-worn and faded.

I ♡ totoro.

don't forget the most important Coca Cola!!

Boy's 3-a-pack boxers — cheap and comfy!! Color faded pastels.

ACTION GIRL GOES TO MOM'S

Thick black stockings — (tights and pantyhose → aggravate those "feminine" problems.)

Baggy shorts made from old men's pants cut off below the knee and rolled up. Multi-colored.

♪ baggy trousers ♪

Vintage day dress, Mom likes it, so does → Action Girl. Any color! Go Nuts!

Hi Mom, let's talk about our boyfriends!! Aren't guys jerks!!

100% cotton boot socks. No blisters!! Color purple →

Action boots! $9 from thrift shop - go with all action outfits and outlast Docs.

dirty socks from never wearing shoes in the house.

OH NO!! ACTION GIRL WAS DRAWN BY A GUY!!

save her now!!

ACTION GIRL GOES SKA!

ACTION GIRL FIGHTS EVIL!

AG's official heroine jacket. Dashing, yet warm and comfy.

"help!"

"help!"

"INSTRUCTIONS: Cut out, then rip up over a trash can while laughing gleefully!!

Crisp white shirt stolen from a boy.

Button- put your favorite band here.

Action Girl hates evil

Short full skirt means freedom of movement!

Like anyone has this body. Do these guys ever have dates? Have they seen a woman's body?

hahahahahahaha

Ties should only come in black

Evilstomping boots give Action Girl extra powers.

Like you can do anything in this cape.

Kicky pleated skirt - dark or a nice plaid.

stomp out all bad!!

Where do these boots come from? Special stores for super-gals and hookers?

♪ ska ska ska ♪

♪ do the ♪ ♪ ska ♪

Rudie hat! Cut on dotted line. Color black and slip over Action Girl's head.

DESIGN A COLOR SCHEME FOR ACTION GIRLS' BATTLES AGAINST EVIL!!

yeah, right!!

so pathetic.

by and © sarah d. 1993

206. An Action Girl paper doll page. Again, Dyer supplies a woman's opinion of male-drawn super-heroines. (*Action Girl Comics* no. 2, January 18, 1995.)

207. Liana uses her powers. (*A Distant Soil,* no. 8, 1994.)

208. Immola, the Hot Ticket, and the Luna Legion. (OH . . . no. 7, 1994.)

blindfolded. C. J. Henderson scripted the first three issues, and then Wendi Lee took over with the story of Sylvia, aka Beauty, a Latina gang member. The very strong antigang message is well written and reminiscent of the film *Mi Vida Loca.* If artist Greg Boone could have restrained himself, this would have made an excellent educational comic book for American high schools. But even though later episodes play down the graphic sex and violence, Boone seems to have been unable to resist giving readers a flash of bare breast and a graphically knocked-out tooth in the first episode, thereby making its acceptance in schools improbable.

Latina and other nonwhite superheroines are still very much in the minority. Milestone, a distinctive comics line published by DC but created mostly by and for people of color, features a good number of African American and Latina superheroines. As with a majority of contemporary superhero comics, most of the women are members of supergroups, but one unusual superheroine stands alone: Rocket. Without his fifteen-year-old sidekick, Rocket, the superhero, Icon, would be merely an African American Superman. Raquel Ervin, Rocket's alter ego, is a superheroine for the nineties with problems of the nineties: she is an unmarried pregnant teenager. Raquel gets her powers from a special belt that she wears and, when she gets too pregnant to fasten the clasp, she gives the costume to her girlfriend, Darnice, who becomes a temporary Rocket. The African American teenage girl is the first superheroine to go on maternity leave.

AC comics, one of America's oldest independent publishers, has specialized since 1982 in producing only superheroine comics, basing their characters on costumed superwomen from the 1940s. Nightveil, Ms. Victory, She-Cat, Synn, Stardust, and Tara each star in their own books, and together are featured in a group comic, *Femforce.* Although they are all drawn with a heavy emphasis on curves, the stories are light-hearted, and happily lack the gore that is a major part of too many contemporary comics. Despite their exaggerated bust sizes, the super-powered heroines wear much more than today's bad girls and, in fact, compared to the bad girl comics, they are positively wholesome.

In 1995, recognizing that many women are put off by the way in which so many modern superheroines have been drawn, AC comics made an offer to its women readers: redesign our heroines for a special issue of *Femforce.* "Women reading comics and those working in the business often complain about the portrayal of female characters," read the copy. "So here's an opportunity you've been waiting for . . . the opportunity to do things your way! You can change the body type of our characters; height, weight, bust sizes, etc. Changes can be made in their hair styles and in their costumes. . . .

209. Panels from *Cyberzone,* **self-published by Jimmy Robinson, starring African American superheroine Amanda Shane. (Top,** *Cyberzone* **no. 1, 1994; bottom,** *Cyberzone* **no. 6, 1995.)**

If you don't like the way today's publishers are portraying female characters, maybe it's time to 'lash back'!"

Since 1982, when Joshua Quagmire started publishing *Cutey Bunny,* self-published comics have been the place to find the most unusual superheroines. Cutey Bunny, whose name is a pun on a Japanese cartoon character called Cutey Honey, is the world's first (and only) African American rabbit superheroine. Quagmire's flying bunny is actually Kelly O'Hare, a corporal in the armed forces. The first issue explains that when Kelly "rubs her Ancient Egyptian amulet which she got from an ancient Egyptian bubble gum machine, in downtown Cairo . . . she is magically transformed into Cutey Bunny (Actually, what really happens is the cartoonist just draws her with a different costume . . .) But don't tell anyone, okay . . . ?"

In the comics industry, self-published comic books have the smallest print runs and are usually printed in black and white, but they are the personal vision of the creator/publisher. Because of this, the superheroines who emerge from the pages of these small-press comics tend to be more original than the bad girl clones or the superteam members put out by larger publishers.

Strange Attractors, self-published by Michael Cohen and Mark Sherman since 1994, is a superheroine comic within a superheroine comic. In a far-distant future on the asteroid Sisyphus, Sophie catalogues rooms in the Museum of Lost Things, aided by her faithful and cute robot, Roshi. Her biggest inspirations are the comics she read as a child, *Spicy Space Stories,* featuring superheroines Nurse Nebula, Pirate Peg, and the Moon Marauders. When she discovers that her best friend is in danger, Sophie and Roshi board a

210. Onca Ray, the on-line woman superheroine.

211. Multi-media artist Ruth Taylor as Onca Ray.

rocket ship and set out to help. Their rocket ship pilot turns out to be none other than her childhood idol, Pirate Peg, and Sophie soon finds herself in the middle of an outer-space adventure where she encounters other heroines from the pages of *Spicy Space Stories. Strange Attractors* is obviously inspired by the forties' *Planet Comics,* but there's a grrrl cuteness about the book that turns it into Betty and Veronica Meet Mysta of the Moon.

Action Girl comics started in 1994, as an outgrowth of Sarah Dyer's 1991 *Action Girl Newsletter.* She describes the newsletter as "a guide to projects produced by girls, grrrls and women. Boy-friendly, but very pro-girl." Her comic is an anthology of work by various young women writer-artists, but Action Girl herself, who appears irregularly in the book, is a spunky young superheroine. Sometimes she interacts with her super-powered friend, Flying Girl, a creation of Elizabeth Watasin. Every issue of the comic book is enlivened with Dyer's Action Girl paper dolls, which reflect her unique thrift-shop fashion theories. Though not always drawn or even written by Dyer, *Action Girl* is a personal vision with universal appeal to young women. Dyer states in her editorial that the book "is wholly my comic, not some publisher's collection of

stuff. . . . The material . . . will always reflect my sensibilities. . . ."

Since 1991, Colleen Doran has been chronicling the adventures of another young girl, Liana, in her self-published *A Distant Soil* in a decorative style, which shows influences of art nouveau artists Alphonse Mucha and Aubrey Beardsley, as

212. The newest Wonder Woman. (*Wonder Woman*, no. 101, 1995.)

well as art deco artist Erte. Doran has drawn for all the major comic book publishers, but *A Distant Soil* is her personal vision, a project she has been working on since the age of twelve. Liana is on the run after an escape from the Martin Institute for Mental Health, where she and her brother Jason had been held since childhood as subjects for psychic phenomena research. Liana amasses a small group of allies against the Institute, including some very beautiful, sexually ambiguous aliens who have come to Earth to recruit humans in their battle against the planet Ovanan, which has subjugated much of the universe. Liana learns that she and Jason are the children of a fugitive from Ovanan, and that she is an Avatar, the most powerful psychic being in the universe. Ovanan's own Avatar, the planet's religious leader and protector, has lost her powers because of Liana's existence on Earth, and the Ovanans will stop at nothing to destroy her. Meanwhile, Jason, who has powers of his own, has been kidnapped by the Ovanans.

Joan Hilty's Lesbian superheroine, Immola, the Hot Ticket, appears regularly in the Canadian magazine *Oh . . . .* Immola belongs to an all-girl supergroup called Luna Legion. Along with the other superheroines, Diabolique, Cuffs,

Sphinx, and their cigar-smoking manager, Kovis, she fights bad guys using a jet pack and her powers of combustion—she can set things on fire. When not battling the forces of evil, Immola has the usual problems of your everyday lesbian superheroine. She tries to pick up a cute woman in a lesbian bar by admitting she's a superheroine—and the woman turns out to be the infamous villainess Black Friday.

The bald heroine of Jimmy Robinson's self-published *Cyberzone* is a lesbian and an African American. Amanda Shane is a "certified superhero," who carries a superhero priority card, working in a dystopic future, along with her robotic talking supergun, Gunn.

In November 1994, the *Los Angeles Times* published a letter from nine-year-old Alexandra Early, of Arlington, Massachusetts, under the headline, "Where Are The Girl Superheroes?" Alexandra writes about superheroines on television, but what she has to say pertains to comic books, too: "I'm a girl and there aren't enough girl superheroes on TV . . . . On *X Man* [sic] there are some strong women but they always need help and they always have to look sexy . . . they wear short dresses and funny bikini tops . . . . It's not fair at all. I want it equal. Like why isn't there a

213. Sophie and The Collector who holds her captive; story by Michael Cohen and Mark Sherman, art by Michael Cohen. (*Strange Attractors* no. 6, August 1994).

214. A final comment by Sarah Dyer. (Cover of *Action Girl* no. 1.)

strong girl who does everything the men do? Why isn't there a show called X Woman as opposed to X Man? . . . I hope the people who make these shows know there are girls like me watching. We want fairness."

Different as they are, the heroines of *Strange Attractors, Immola, Action Girl, A Distant Soil,* and *Cyberzone* have much in common: they all wear enough clothes, they never wind up covered in blood, they are girl-friendly, they are nice. Alexandra Early would like them very much.

As modern as they get is *Onca Ray,* an on-line superheroine for the computer age. Created by multimedia artist Ruth Taylor (who gives live performances as her character) and drawn by her father, Tom Taylor, the part–New Age, part–pop art heroine from ancient Egypt can be visited on her own World Wide Web site.

In 1995, John Byrne took over the art and writing of *Wonder Woman* and revised the world's most famous superheroine one more time. He redesigned her costume, giving her a bit more than the thong bikini in which Mike Deodato had put her; she no longer looks like a fugitive from *Penthouse.* Invoking the spirit of Harry G. Peter, Byrne has given the Amazon princess thick, curly, Mediterranean hair; a strong, well-defined chin; and the slim, muscular body of an Olympic swimming champion. William Moulton Marston would approve.

NOTES

CHAPTER ONE

1) Marston's 1943 article about the reasoning that went into his creation: Marston, W. M. 1943-44. "Why 100,000,000 Americans Read Comics." *The American Scholar.* Winter.

2) "The early Wonder Woman scripts were a family affair . . .": From a telephone interview with Pete Marston.

3) Princess Diana's origin, and her rescue of Steve Trevor, were retold more than once. A good classic version can be found in *Wonder Woman* no. 1, Summer 1942. Similar versions appeared in *All Star* and in *Sensation.*

4) Queen Atomia's story: *Wonder Woman* no. 21, 1947.

5) Olive Norton's story: *Sensation Comics,* 1946.

6) "This set the theme for future writers, like Jim Harmon . . .": Harmon, J. 1970. "A Swell Bunch of Guys." *All in Color For A Dime.* p.186.

7) "James Steranko states . . .": Steranko, J. 1970. *The Steranko History of Comics,* vol. 1, p. 71.

8) "And Richard Reynolds . . . goes so far as to write . . .": Reynolds, R. 1992. *Super Heroes, a Modern Mythology.* p 34.

9) Queen Hippolyta expresses the humanitarian theme: *Wonder Woman* no. 32, 1948.

10) "Writer Les Daniels is aware of this . . .": Daniels, L. 1971. *Comix, A History of Comic Books in America.* p. 13.

11) "One wonders if it is not the same standard . . .": Feiffer, J. 1965. *The Great Comic Book Heroes.* pp. 44–45.

12) Gloria Steinem introduction: Steinem, G. 1972. Introduction to *Wonder Woman.*

CHAPTER TWO

1) "In fact, Mills had changed her first name . . .": Aronson, J. "Meet The Real Miss Fury— It's All Done With Mirrors," (sent to author by Donald Goldsamt. Unfortunately, name and date of newspaper had been trimmed off).

2) Tarpe Mills and her cat make headlines: *Miami Daily News.* 1945.

3) "In 1943, even Time got into the act . . .": *Time.* 1943. p. 27.

4) "Her first adventure . . ." *Eagle Comics* no. 2. September 1941.

5) "The last panel of . . .": *Comedy Comics* no. 9. April 1942.

6) "In the story . . .": "Crimes of Catwoman." *Detective Comics* no. 203. January 1953.

CHAPTER THREE

1) "At least six months . . .": *Feature Comics* no. 45. 1941.

2) "Commandette only appeared in one issue . . .": Actually there only was one issue of *Star Studded Comics!* She appeared in that issue.

3) "Two years later . . .": *Dynamic Comics* no. 23. November 1947.

4) "That first issue also featured a subscription blank . . .": Author's telephone interview with Vincent Fago.

5)"This leads to confusing scenes . . .": *Speed Comics* no. 19. May 1942.

6) "One of the more dramatic stories . . .": *Airfighters* no. 11. August 1943.

7) "In the last panel of one of her adventures . . .": *Great Comics* no. 3, 1942.

CHAPTER FOUR

1) "Flame Girl, who can burst into flame . . .": *Wonderworld Comics* no. 33. 1942.

2) "Catman, who had his own comic book . . .": The Kitten was not really a blood relative of Catman's, though she referred to him as "uncle." When she was first introduced in the comic, in *Catman* no. 5, December 1941, she

NOTES

was an orphan, traveling with her "Uncle Jake," a thief. Catman rescued her from the brutal uncle, and she helped him break up a nest of Nazi spies.

3) "Marc Swayze remembers . . .": Author's telephone interview with Marc Swayze.

4) Mary Marvel tackles the boy's club: *Wow Comics* no. 39. November–December 1945

5) Mary Marvel fashions: *Wow Comics* no. 56, 1947.

CHAPTER FIVE

1) "In a 1942 story . . .": *Dynamic Comics* no. 3. February 1942.

2) "Unfortunately, Ghost Woman only made one appearance . . .": There was only one issue of *Star Studded Comics,* remember?

3) "Artist Jim Mooney, just out of art school . . .": Author's telephone interview with Jim Mooney.

4) "A story in . . .": *Smash* no. 36. October 1942.

5) Magga the Magnificent: *Atoman* no. 2. April 1946.

6) Lucille Martin is given a mystic blue stone: *Amazing Man* no. 24. October 1941.

7) Maggie Thompson's fascination with Moon Girl: Author's telephone interview with Maggie Thompson.

8) "According to her very romantic origin . . .": *Moon Girl and the Prince* no. 1. 1947.

9) "Moldoff based the princess's exotic looks . . .": Letter by Sheldon Moldoff.

10) "When a mysterious box arrives . . .": *Planet Comics* no. 55. July 1948.

CHAPTER SIX

1) "Atoma, who appeared only once . . .": *Joe Palooka* no. 15. December 1947.

2) "In a short comic story . . .": "I Hate Me." Lee, S. 1947. *Secrets Behind the Comics.* p. 48.

3) "Although in issue no. 1, she briefly carries an emergency pouch . . .": *Sun Girl* no. 1. August 1948.

4) "Venus's first story . . .": *Venus* no. 1. August 1948.

5) ". . . the last issue of Venus comics . . .": *Venus* no. 19. April 1952.

CHAPTER SEVEN

1) The postwar decline of superheroes has been chronicled by many authors including: Daniel, L. 1991. *Marvel;* Goulart, R. 1986. Chapter 17. *Great History of Comic Books.* pp. 241ff.; Benton, M. 1992. *Superhero Comics of the Golden Age.* p. 57.

2) Tomboy vs. The Claw: *Captain Flash* no. 1. November 1954.

3) "Then, in a special issue of Action comics . . .": *Action* no. 285. February 1962.

4) "In fact, Jim Mooney remembers . . .": Author's telephone interview with Jim Mooney.

5) "A 1964 Supergirl story . . .": *Action* no. 311. April 1964.

6) "A 1963 Wonder Woman letters page . . .": *Wonder Woman* no. 138. May 1963.

7) "Meanwhile, Marvel . . . had fared even worse . . .": Daniels, L. 1991. *Marvel.* p. 80; Evanier, M. 1995 "Point Of View." *The Comics Buyer's Guide.* no. 1123. May 26. p.50.

CHAPTER EIGHT

1) Invisible Girl's hobbies: *Fantastic Four Annual* no. 1. 1963.

2) "In contrast to the all-girl letter page . . .": *The Avengers* no. 16. May 1965.

3) "The Mighty Marvel Checklist . . .": Compare

this to a list of comics published by Marvel which appeared in all of their comic books in 1948, the year of the Great Superheroine Slumber Party. Of forty-nine comic books listed, twenty-six of them—more than half—were of obvious appeal to women and girls. Seventeen of those boasted a female name in the title, such as Annie Oakley, Sun Girl, Blonde Phantom, Tessie the Typist, etc. That same year, a study made in New Orleans (*Report on Comic Books.* October 18, 1948. p. 5) found that in the age group twenty-one to thirty, 42.9 percent of the men and a whopping 51 percent of the women were comic book readers.

4) "Letters to the *Teen Titans* show that readers were already hopelessly confused . . ." *Teen Titans* nos. 20 and 21. April and June 1969.

5) "She wasn't an Amazon after all.": *Teen Titans* no. 22. August 1969.

6)"Most of the letters pages included at least one letter from a girl.": *Teen Titans* no. 24. December 1969.

7) "Batgirl's Costume Cut-ups": *Detective Comics* no. 371. January 1968.

CHAPTER NINE

1) "Come on in . . . the Revolution's Fine": *Avengers* no. 83. December 1970.

2) "Thus, in 1971, Shirley A. Gorman . . . wrote . . .": *Amazing Adventures* no. 8. September 1971.

3) Linda Fite remembers: Author's telephone interview with Linda Fite.

4) "At the beginning of 1973, Bill Everett . . .": *Submariner* no. 57. January 1973.

5) "Roy Thomas insists . . .": Author's telephone interviews with Roy Thomas and Stan Lee.

6) "She accomplishes her magic by making up poetry . . .": *The Mighty Isis* no. 1.

November 1976.

7) The romance of Azrael and Lilith: *The New Teen Titans* no. 29. 1983.

8) "The year 1982 found her romantically involved with one of the X-Men.": *Dazzler* no. 17. July 1982.

CHAPTER TEN

1) "As can be seen on the letters pages . . .": *Amethyst, Princess of Gemworld* no. 11. 1983.

2) "I filled in with a four-part limited series . . .": *The Legend of Wonder Woman* nos. 1–4. 1986.

CHAPTER ELEVEN

1) "When her supervisor yells": *Wonder Woman* no. 76. July 1993. Incidentally, Lee Moder, the artist on this issue, drew probably the best Wonder Woman since Harry G. Peter. Themiscyra, or what had once been called Paradise Island, had a habit of disappearing into another dimension or being destroyed, then popping back up again when convenient. This had happened back in 1968, and would happen again in 1995, when John Byrne took over the book.

2) "Later that year they canceled their last superheroine book . . .": In January 1996, Marvel began a Storm miniseries. But they do not currently publish any regular continuing superheroine titles.

3) "Their excuse . . . is that 'women don't read comics'": However, in the past, when there were a good many more comic books that appealed to female readers, they read comics in great numbers. A 1946 graph in *Newsdealer* shows that in the age groups eight to eleven and eighteen to thirty-four, female comic book readers exceeded the males (*Newsdealer.* April, 1946). A 1955 study undertaken in Dayton, Ohio, shows that in the age group eight to fourteen, 96.5 percent and 94.7 percent of the girls read comic books (Feder, E. L. 1955. *Comic*

Book Regulation. p. 2). See also notes for Chapter Eight.

4) Controversy over Catwoman's new look: *Comics Buyer's Guide.* no. 107. October 1, 1993. Female readers also expressed their feelings about the new Wonder Woman, as drawn by Mike Deodato, in the letters pages of the *Wonder Woman* comic book. In issue no. 95, March 1995, Kate Payne, of Myrtle Point, Oregon, wrote: "That thong-back look is not flattering. I realize it may be some slobbering male's idea of a wet dream, but in reality, it's tacky. Right there, page 1, we are treated to a spectacular view of Diana's rear. No class. Again, on page 15, same view. Glancing through the entire comic, every woman's cheeks are out flapping in the breeze. C'mon, give them some coverage and some dignity." Joanna Sandsmark, of Studio City, California, wrote in the same letters page: "Personally, it's a little heavy on the T&A for me, but then, I'm female and that's to be expected. . . . Please get Diana out of her slutty new outfit. . . Did Circe cast a spell to infuse the fashion sense of a hooker in Diana's mind?" Editor Paul Kupperberg's answer? "You've got to learn to relax and go with the flow, Joanna. . . ."

5) "The 92 percent male comic book readership of the nineties . . .": *DC Comics Survey,* conducted by Mark Clements Research, 1994, lists 92.2 percent male readership. *A Survey of Young Upwardly Mobile Men,* conducted by Mediamark Research Inc. in 1992, lists 93.1 percent male readership on page 4. Later, on page 41, the survey states that ". . . 65 female respondents were removed prior to tabulation."

6) "When writer Lee Marrs revived the magician Zatanna . . .": *Zatanna* no. 2, August 1993.

7) Sarah Byam and Black Canary: Byam made an interesting discovery about comics and their readers in 1995 when she taught a comics class for children in Seattle. She had a pile of comic books from the major publishers which she gave away to the students and their younger siblings. She found that the boys chose comics with male leads (the majority of the books), and that the girls chose those few comics with "girl" appeal, like *Barbie* or *Silver Sable,* but that when the small supply of "girl" comics was used up, the girls simply stopped taking comics. When there are comics for them to read, girls do read comics.

8) ". . . angry letters from male readers": *Black Canary* no. 12. 1992.

9) "Comics Journalist Kurt Samuels describes bad girl comics . . .": Samuels, K. 1995. "Market Report." *Entertainment Edition.* p. 14.

10) "When the popular superhero, Spawn, is brought to Elysium . . .": *Angela* no. 2. January 1995.

11) "In one story, Martha finds herself in the middle of a civil war . . .": *Happy Birthday, Martha Washington.* March 1995.

12) ". . . and then Wendi Lee took over, with the story of Sylvia . . .": *Lady Justice* nos. 4–6. December 1995–January 1996.

13) "In 1995, recognizing that many women are put off . . .": *Femforce* no. 86. 1995.

14) "In November 1994, the *Los Angeles Times* published a letter . . .": Actually, Alexandra Early's letter was first printed in the *Arlington Advocate* (January 27, 1994). In an article written by Gwenn Mercadoocasio, Heidi MacDonald, comics editor of *Disney Adventures,* quotes a letter which she received from another eleven-year-old girl: "You know, I really love the X-Men, but they never put Rogue and Storm in enough. How come they don't have them in the ads? . . . Even though I'm just 11 years old, I think it's kind of sexist." ("Who's Responsible For This Stuff Anyhow?" *Comics Values Monthly* no. 97. 1994. p. 115.)

BIBLIOGRAPHY

Aronson, James. "Meet The Real Miss Fury—It's All Done With Mirrors," N.d. n.p. Undated newspaper clipping.

Bails, Jerry and Hames Ware, eds. *Who's Who of American Comic Books,* volumes 1–4. St. Claire Shores, Michigan: Jerry Bails, 1973–1976.

Benton, Mike. *The Comic Book in America: An Illustrated History.* Dallas: Taylor Publishing Company, 1989.

_____. *Science Fiction Comics, The Illustrated History.* Dallas, Texas: Taylor Publishing Company, 1992.

_____. *Superhero Comics of the Silver Age: The Illustrated History.* Dallas: Taylor Publishing Company, 1991.

_____. *Superhero Comics of the Golden Age: The Illustrated History.* Dallas: Taylor Publishing Company, 1992.

Blackbeard, Bill and Dale Crain, eds. *The Comic Strip Century.* 2 vols. Northampton, Massachusetts: Kitchen Sink Press, 1995.

Comics Buyer's Guide no. 107. "Oh, So!" and passim. October 1, 1993.

Couperie, Pierre and Maurice C. Horn. *A History of the Comic Strip.* Translated by Eileen B. Hennessy. New York: Crown Publishers, Inc., 1974.

Crawford, Huberth H. *Crawford's Encyclopedia of Comic Books.* Middle Village, New York: Jonathan David Publisher's Inc., 1978.

Daniels, Les. *Comix, A History of Comic Books in America.* New York: Bonanza Books, 1971.

_____. *Marvel: Five Fabulous Decades of the World's Greatest Comics.* New York: Harry N. Abrams, Inc., 1991.

Evanier, Mark. "Point of View." *The Comics Buyer's Guide* no. 1123, May 26, 1995.

Everett, Bill. "Everett on Everett." *Alter Ego* no. 11. 1978.

Faludi, Susan. *Backlash.* New York: Crown Publishers, Inc., 1991.

Feder, Edward L., comp. *Comic Book Regulation.* Berkeley: University of California, Bureau of Public Administration. 1955.

Feiffer, Jules. *The Great Comic Book Heroes.* New York: Dial Press, 1965.

Friedan, Betty, *The Feminine Mystique.* New York: Dell, 1974 [1963].

BIBLIOGRAPHY

Gerber, Ernst. *The Photo-Journal Guide to Comic Books.* 2 volumes. Minden, Nevada: Gerber Publishing Co., 1989–1990.

_____. *The Photo-Journal Guide to Marvel Comics.* 2 volumes. Minden, Nevada: Gerber Publishing Co., 1991.

Gifford, Denis. *The International Book of Comics.* New York: Crescent Books, 1984.

Goulart, Ron. *Great History of Comic Books.* Chicago: Contemporary Books, 1986.

_____. *The Encyclopedia of American Comics.* New York: Facts on File Publications, 1990.

_____. *The Comic Book Reader's Companion, An A-to-Z Guide to Everyone's Favorite Art Form.* New York: HarperPerennial, 1993.

Harmon, Jim. "A Swell Bunch of Guys." In Lupoff and Thompson, eds, *All In Color For A Dime.* Arlington House, 1970.

Jacobs, Will and Gerard Jones. *The Comic Book Heroes.* New York: Crown, 1985.

Keaton, Russell. *The Aviation Art of Russell Keaton.* Foreword by Loretta Gragg; introduction by Deborah Brunt. Northampton, Massachusetts: Kitchen Sink Press, 1995.

Korkis, Jim. "Wild Bill: That Man from Atlantis." *Golden Age of Comics* no. 8, February 1984.

Kurtzman, Harvey. *From Aargh! to Zap!; Harvey Kurtzman's Visual History of the Comics.* New York: Prentice Hall Press, 1991.

Lee, Stan. *Secrets Behind the Comics.* Famous Enterprises, Inc., 1947.

Lupoff, Dick [Richard] and Don[ald] Thompson, *All in Color for a Dime.* New Rochelle, New York: Arlington House, 1970.

Mark Clements Research. *DC Comics Survey.* 1994.

Marston, William Moulton. "Why 100,000,000 Americans Read Comics." *The American Scholar.* Winter, 1943-44.

Mediamark Research Inc. *A Survey of Young Upwardly Mobile Men.* 1992.

Mercadoocasio, Gwenn. "Who's Responsible For This Stuff Anyhow?" *Comics Values Monthly* no. 97, 1994.

O'Brien, Richard. *The Golden Age of Comic Books.* New York: Ballantine Books, 1977.

BIBLIOGRAPHY

O'Sullivan, Judith. *The Great American Comic Strip: One Hundred Years of Cartoon Art.* New York: Bulfinch Press, 1990.

Reed, Rod. Interview. *Comics Interview* no. 18, December 1984.

Report on Comic Books. New Orleans Public Relations Section, October 18, 1948.

Reynolds, Richards. *Superheroes, A Modern Mythology.* Jackson, Mississippi: University of Mississippi Press, 1992.

Robbins, Trina. *A Century of Women Cartoonists.* Northampton, Massachusetts: Kitchen Sink Press, 1993.

_____ and catherine yronwode. *Women and the Comics.* Np.: Eclipse Books, 1985.

Robinson, Jerry. *The Comics: An Illustrated History of Comic Strip Art.* New York: G. P. Putnam's Sons, 1974.

Rothschild, Aviva D. *Graphic Novels: A Bibliographic Guide to Book-length Comics.* Englewood, Colorado: Libraries Unlimited, Inc., 1995.

Rovin, Jeff. *The Encyclopedia of Superheroes.* New York: Facts on File Publications, 1985.

Sabin, Roger. *Adult Comics: An Introduction.* New York: Routlege, 1993.

Samuels, Kurt. "Market Report." *Entertainment Edition.* December 8, 1995.

Scott, Randall W. *Comic Books and Strips: An Information Sourcebook.* Phoenix, Arizona: Onyx Press, 1988.

Simon, Joe with Jim Simon. *The Comic Book Makers.* New York: Crestwood/II Publications, 1990.

Steinham, Gloria. Introduction to *Wonder Woman.* New York, Chicago, and San Francisco: Holt, Rinehart, and Winston and Warner Books, 1972.

Steranko, Jim. *The Steranko History of Comics,* volumes 1 and 2. Reading, Pennsylvania: Supergraphics, 1970–1972.

Strickler, Dave, comp. *Syndicated Comic Strips and Artists,1924–1995: The Complete Index.* Grover Beach, California: Comics Access, 1995.

Waugh, Coulton. *The Comics.* New York: The Macmillan Company, 1947.

Wertham, Fredric. *Seduction of the Innocent.* New York: Rinehart and Company, 1954.

IDENTIFICATION KEY

TO THE SUPERHEROINES ON THE COVER'S BACKGROUND; ALSO REPRODUCED ON PAGES 204–205

Reading left to right on pages 204–205:

Top row: the Woman in Red; Rocketgirl; sound effects from Lady Fairplay; the Black Angel; Yankee Girl; and Miss Fury.

Second row: the Blue Lady; Miss Masque; Bulletgirl; Miss Victory; Femforce; Black Venus; Pat Patriot; and Immola.

Third row: Onca Ray; Miss Fury; Martha Washington; Lady Fairplay; Super Ann; Miss Victory; Kitten.

Bottom row: top, Ghost Woman, bottom, Super Ann, Black Widow, Atoma; top, Lois, bottom, the Spider Queen, Lady Satan, Miss Fury, Rocketgirl, Heartbreakers, and the Spider Queen.

The four costumed superheroines appearing in color on the front cover and above in black and white are, left to right: Miss Masque, Phantom Lady, Lady Luck, and Moon Girl.

FIFTY-ODD YEARS OF SUPERHEROINES: A TIMELINE

1939

Germany invades Poland.

Britain and France declare war on Germany.

All that year, William Moulton Marston has a special display featuring his lie detector at the New York World's Fair. He and publisher Max Gaines have already begun discussing the creation of a female superhero named Diana.

1940

France falls to Germany.

The German bombing of London (the Blitz) begins.

The Woman in Red, the first costumed action heroine, begins in *Thrilling Comics.*

1941

April: Miss Fury, the first major costumed action heroine—and the only one created by a woman, Tarpe Mills—makes her debut in newspapers.

August: Black Cat, the first major costumed action heroine in comic books, debuts in *Pocket Comics* no. 1. These two superheroines, along with USA, Pat Patriot, and Miss Victory, all fight Nazis, although the United States is not yet officially at war.

December: Wonder Woman, written by William Moulton Marston under the pseudonym Charles Moulton, makes her first appearance in *All Star Comics* no. 8.

December: Japan bombs Pearl Harbor; the United States enters World War II.

The Women's Auxiliary Ferrying Squadron (WAFS) is formed, for women pilots with 500 hours of flying time.

Real women have entered the war, becoming real life super-heroines.

Mary Marvel debuts in *Captain Marvel Adventures* no. 18.

1943

All women pilots, including the WAFS, become known as Women's Airforce Service Pilots (WASP).

1944

With victory in Europe in sight, the WASPS are disbanded. Wonder Woman, Miss Fury, Black Cat, Pat Patriot, Miss Victory, Liberty Belle, Miss America, the Girl Commandos, and all their patriotic supersisters continue to fight.

1945

America A-bombs Hiroshima and Nagasaki, ending World War II.

Mary Marvel gets her own comic book.

1946

Phantom Lady, who had been around in a slightly less glamorous form since 1941, gets a new publisher, Fox, and a new look from glamour artist par excellence, Matt Baker.

Another important phantom superheroine, Blonde Phantom, also originates this year, created by Stan Lee for the Marvel Comics Group.

A graph in *Newsdealer* magazine shows that in the age group eight to eleven years, and the age group eighteen to thirty-four years, female comic book readers outnumber male readers.

1947

William Moulton Marston dies. Harry G. Peter continues to draw *Wonder Woman.*

Max Gaines, apparently regretting that he let National Comics have Wonder Woman, publishes *Moon Girl.*

1948

Namora, Sun Girl, and Venus join Blonde Phantom at the Marvel Comics Group, becoming a unique group of four superheroines, each starring in her own book, each created specifically for a female audience.

A survey made in New Orleans shows that in the age group twenty-one to thirty, women outnumber men as comic book readers.

1949

The end of Phantom Lady, Miss Masque, and Blonde Phantom.

Depending on which newspaper carried her, *Miss Fury* ends in 1949 or 1950.

1950

Senator Joseph McCarthy launches a campaign to expose alleged Communists in the State Department. This marks the start of the anti-Communist hysteria of the fifties.

1951

Black Canary has her last adventure in *All Star Comics.*

1952

Venus ends.

1954

The end of Mary Marvel.

The publication of Fredric Wertham's *Seduction of the Innocent* at an already-paranoid time in the United States adds fear of the comic book menace to fear of the Red menace. A Senate subcommittee is formed to look into the dangers of comic books, and the majority of comic book publishers fold.

1955

Namora, the last survivor of Stan Lee's group of four super-heroines, has her last adventure in *Submariner.*

Wonder Woman is the only surviving superheroine in comics.

1959

In *Action Comics* no. 252, a rocket bearing Superman's cousin, Kara, lands on Earth. She becomes Supergirl.

1960

The United States gets a new president and first lady—Jack and Jackie Kennedy—and enters a new era.

Wonder Woman also enters a new era; Robert Kanigher, writer and editor for *Wonder Woman,* tosses out her origin as created by William Moulton Marston, and creates Wonder Tot and Wonder Girl.

1961

Cosmic rays turn Reed Richards, Ben Grimm, and Johnny and Sue Storm into the supergroup, the Fantastic Four. Sue Storm becomes Invisible Girl—and faints a lot.

1963

John Fitzgerald Kennedy is assassinated.

The Feminine Mystique by Betty Friedan is published, causing many women to sharply question their traditional roles as wives and mothers.

Jean Grey (Marvel Girl) of the newly-created X-Men does

not question her traditional role. Like Invisible Girl, she faints a lot when she isn't shopping.

1966

The National Organization for Women (NOW) is formed. One of its founders is Betty Friedan.

1968

Women demonstrate at the Miss America Pageant in Atlantic City, and disrupt a live telecast of the contest. This is the first mass action of what was then called the Women's Liberation Movement.

Women's Liberation has not yet reached the comics. Wonder Woman loses her powers, puts on Mod clothing, and opens a boutique. Meanwhile, the cover of *Detective Comics* shows Batgirl refusing to help Batman and Robin fight the bad guys because she has run in her tights.

1970

Women's Liberation, in a slightly wonky form, finally reaches the Marvel bullpen. In a story titled "Come on in . . . the Revolution's Fine," a new character named Valkyrie leads the women members of the Avengers in a revolt against the male members. Her "war cry" is "Up against the wall, male chauvinist pigs!"

Black Widow stars in eight issues of *Amazing Adventures*. She is the first marvel superheroine to star in her own series since the demise of Venus.

1972

The first issue of *Ms. Magazine* appears, with Wonder Woman on the cover.

Valkyrie returns to Marvel Comics, now as a member of the Defenders.

Stan Lee comes up with three comics, all with female protagonists, all aimed at a female audience. One is a superheroine: the Cat.

1976

Superheroines like Wonder Woman and Mighty Isis are now on television. DC Comics publishes a *Mighty Isis* comic book.

1977

Marvel Comics adds Ms. Marvel to their growing list of superheroines who star in their own books.

1978

Spider-Woman debuts at Marvel.

1980

Ronald Reagan elected president. He promises to bring prosperity back to the United States by "getting the government off our backs."

Jennifer Walters gets a blood transfusion from her cousin, Bruce Banner, aka the Hulk, and becomes the Savage She-Hulk.

1981

Reagan is inaugurated. He cuts programs for the environment and the regulation of business by forty-three billion dollars and makes massive increases in the defense budget.

1982

The first Rambo movie, *First Blood*, echoes the prevailing political mood.

The first major new superheroine of the eighties also echoes the country's mood—she is Elektra, a professional assassin.

1983

United States armed forces commence what will turn out to be a series of invasions of smaller countries in order to take citizens' minds off massive unemployment and justify the military buildup. The first country to be invaded is Grenada.

1985

Reagan inaugurated for a second term.

Dagger, the female half of the vigilante team, Cloak and Dagger, reflects the mood of the day by taking the law into her own hands. Her justification for killing people is simply that they are bad.

1986

The Iran-Contra affair is revealed in the media. It is disclosed that the United States had secretly sold arms to Iran, and that some of the profits had been diverted to aid the U.S.-friendly Nicaraguan Contra rebels against the anti-U.S., democratically elected Nicaraguan government.

The United States bombs Libya.

The June 2 issue of *Newsweek* declares that single women "are more likely to be killed by a terrorist" than to marry.

Throughout the eighties, the mass media have been pushing a return to the traditional role of wife and mother for women.

1989

George Bush is inaugurated president, with Dan Quayle as his vice-president.

The United States invades Panama.

1991

Operation Desert Storm: the United States attacks Iraq to defend oil interests in Kuwait, a country where women do not have the vote; in fact, Kuwaiti women are veiled from head to toe and not even allowed to drive.

Backlash by Susan Faludi is published. It describes how antifeminist backlash in the eighties has worked to undermine the gains attained by women in the seventies.

1992 to date

Bill Clinton, a Democrat with an openly feminist spouse, is elected president of the United States.

The Reaganism/Ramboism and antifeminist backlash of the eighties continue in comics, with the advent of "bad girl" comics—portrayals of hypersexualized women as blood-soaked killers—and the cancellation of more superheroine books.

Not surprisingly, female readership continues to drop. A 1994 DC Comics survey lists 92.9% male readership, versus 5.9% female readership.

At the same time, more positive women heroes emerge from less mainstream comic publishers. These include the British Tank Girl; Martha Washington, from Dark Horse Comics; Joan Hilty's and Jimmie Robinson's lesbian superheroines; and Sarah Dyer's grrrl-friendly Action Girl, among others. Where superheroines will go in the future is anybody's guess.

THE DEFINITIVE HISTORY OF WOMEN IN CARTOONING!

A CENTURY OF WOMEN CARTOONISTS

BY TRINA ROBBINS

A lively visual history of women in cartooning from the early years of this century to the present. Features work from Grace Dayton (*Campbell Kids*) to Nell Brinkley, Rose O'Neill (*The Kewpies*), Dale Messick (*Brenda Starr*), Lynn Johnston (*For Better or Worse*), Carol Lay, Lynda Barry and many, many more.

184 pages, b&w with color covers. Softcover or limited edition hardcover signed by author Trina Robbins, Marie Severin, Dale Messick, Ramona Fradon and Marty Links.

Educational yet entertaining, richly illustrated and filled with unusual facts, Robbins' well-researched book traces the history of cartooning women from the late 1800s through the present. . . . *A Century of Women Cartoonists* highlights the hitherto unknown talent that has added a distinct perspective and significant contribution to pop culture for many decades. —*Bay Guardian*

This book should anger and inspire girl closet scribblers into knowing that their doodles are as much a part of the feminist movement as political speeches. —*Sassy*

A Century of Women Cartoonists manages to examine the greater history of women in the 20th century while keeping a clear focus on the subject at hand. . . . As a historical study, *Century* ends up telling us as much about the evolution (or de-evolution) of cartooning as it does about the women who practiced it. —*Hero Illustrated*

KITCHEN SINK PRESS ®

Available in finer comic shops and bookstores.

The Aviation Art of Russell Keaton

The Aviation Art of Russell Keaton reproduces original art from the finest *Flyin' Jenny* strips plus photographs and unpublished works. Also includes an introduction by journalist and Keaton family friend Deborah P. Brunt, a selection of over one hundred of the artist's letters, and a preface by Loretta Gragg, Executive Director of The Ninety-Nines, Inc., International Women Pilots. This 9 inch by 12 inch volume includes over 150 Sunday and daily comic strips, 40 rare photographs and drawings, and an eight-page color section. *The Aviation Art of Russell Keaton* was published in conjunction with an exhibition of original comic strip art by Russell Keaton for *Flyin' Jenny* at the Oklahoma Air and Space Museum, co-sponsored by Kitchen Sink Press and The Ninety-Nines, Inc., International Women Pilots.

Russell Keaton was a pilot, a flight instructor for the Army Air Corps in World War II, and the cartoonist who drew the most exciting aviation and science fiction comics in the Golden Age of adventure strips—*Buck Rogers*, *Skyroads*, and his masterpiece *Flyin' Jenny*, the only comic strip starring a woman aviator. *Flyin' Jenny* originally appeared in newspapers between 1939 and 1946. The comic strip's heroine was Jenny Dare, a strong, beautiful, and witty woman aviator modeled after Keaton's wife, Virginia. *Flyin' Jenny* featured thrilling stories of stunt flying, adventure, romance, and serious stories about the struggles of women aviators to find their place in the skies.

Available in finer comic shops and bookstores.

For a FREE catalog filled with comics, books and more from the best cartoonists in the world, call 1-800-672-7862, e-mail kitchensp@aol.com, fax 1-413-582-7116, or write Kitchen Sink Press, Inc., 320 Riverside Drive, Northampton, MA 01060.

Trina Robbins's story is a list of firsts. In 1970, she put together the very first all-woman comic book, *It Ain't Me, Babe,* and in 1972, she was one of the founding mothers of the Wimmen's Comix Collective, which produced the longest-running, all-woman anthology comic book. In 1985, she was coauthor of *Women and the Comics* (with cat yronwode), the first book about women working in the comics industry, and in 1993 she published *A Century of Women Cartoonists,* the first book about the women artists and writers who have created comics over the past one hundred years. In 1988, Robbins coedited *Strip AIDS USA,* an AIDS benefit book, and in 1990 she self-published and edited *Choices,* a prochoice benefit book for the National Organization for Women (NOW). Robbins is also the writer and illustrator of a children's book, *Catswalk* (1990); a CD rom for girls, *Hawaii High* (1993); a volume on vintage fashion; and five paper doll books. She has also written and drawn more comic books than she can remember. She has received awards from Parents' Choice, the San Diego Comic Convention, San Francisco NOW, and the San Francisco Media Alliance. She has also produced one beautiful, grown-up daughter, and lives in San Francisco with another cartoonist and entirely too many cats.